W9-BEO-576

FIRST FRUITS

FROM PROMISE TO PROVISION

PAULA WHITE

PUBLISHED BY PAULA WHITE MINISTRIES – TAMPA, FLORIDA

Copyright © 2006 by Paula White
Published by Paula White Ministries, Inc.,
P.O. Box 25151, Tampa, Florida, 33622.

Cover and interior design by Roark Creative, www.roarkcreative.com.

ISBN 978-0-9792092-0-8 (hardback)
ISBN 978-0-9792092-1-5 (paperback)

Unless otherwise indicated, all scripture references are taken from the Holy Bible, King James Version. The King James Version is public domain in the United States.

Scripture quotations marked (NIV) are taken from the HOLY BIBLE, NEW INTERNATIONAL VERSION®. NIV®. Copyright © 1973, 1978, 1984, by International Bible Society. Used by permission of Zondervan. All rights reserved.

Scripture quotations marked (NASB) are taken from the New American Standard Bible®, Copyright © 1960, 1962, 1963, 1968, 1971, 1972, 1973, 1975, 1977, 1995 by The Lockman Foundation. Used by permission. (www.Lockman.org)

Scripture quotations marked (AMP) are taken from the Amplified Bible ®, Copyright © 1954, 1958, 1962, 1964, 1965, 1987 by The Lockman Foundation. Used by permission. (www.Lockman.org)

Scripture quotations marked "NKJV™" are taken from the New King James Version® Copyright 1982 by Thomas Nelson, Inc. Used by permission. All rights reserved.

FIRST FRUITS

FROM PROMISE TO PROVISION

TABLE OF CONTENTS

FOREWORD

First and foremost, I want to give all glory and honor to God. I cannot begin to express or articulate the depth of love and appreciation I feel, or the value it holds, that He has not only seen fit to find and save me, but to reveal Himself and walk me through the destined life He chose for me. I give endless thanks for the blessing of the promise made to us in John 10:10: *"I am come that they might have life, and that they might have [it] more abundantly."* Through Him I have discovered "that life"!!!

My journey for study was not "how" to preach a sermon, or to teach someone else about God; it was out of a deep hunger to know Him. From that hunger I discovered the depth and richness of His Word, and its transformational power when applied to your life. It is this "faith food," that fed and sustained me through the vicissitudes and different seasons of life, that I am now privileged to serve others with. As Ephesians 3:20 declares: *"Now Unto Him that is able to do exceeding abundantly above all that we ask or think, according to the power that worketh in us."*

One of the 'truths' that transformed me was the principle of First Fruits. It is with great honor that I share

His revelation to me: the discovery of His patterns found in the offering First Fruits. The undeniable fact is that *His principles propel you into His promises.* Get ready for great joy on this journey; may it open the eyes of your understanding, and help put you in alignment with God, releasing and manifesting what He has in store for you!

The patterns of God were established long before man had a revelation and saw a manifestation. I see the landscape of your future about to change; I see things looking a whole lot better in every area of your life, as you align yourself with this pattern of God.

I must express my gratitude for all my family, friends, and co-laborers – and all those who dedicate their life, time and talents to carrying forth the vision and sharing the call with me. Thank you! A dream isn't birthed without a team – thank you for calling the vision forth. May your labor of love be richly rewarded.

INTRODUCTION

A PROMISE TO COME...

Promises tend to mean very little in this world. It is sad, but most of us have experienced the disappointment of broken promises far too often to believe promises are more than just empty words.

But I want to remind you that *there is One* who never breaks His promises—God. It is that fact that compels me to share with you the truth behind a powerful "promise to come" in God's Word.

The promise I'm talking about is wrapped up in a principle of faith and obedience that God established from the beginning. This principle called "first fruits" or in Hebrew, *bikkurim,* literally means "a promise to come." Though the Body of Christ has frequently overlooked it today, as you'll see in the following pages, God is faithful to His Word, and will teach us when we have a willing and obedient heart. That is how the revelation began to take hold in my life.

Before I fully comprehended the power behind this principle, the Lord was leading and directing me to walk in it. My life has been blessed because God is faithful to His promises when I am faithful to operate in His order of things. Likewise, many in our church family at Without Walls and around the world who have begun to apply this teaching to their lives are enjoying the benefits

of walking in this spiritual truth!

So I invite you to spend a few hours with me as I begin laying a very simple foundation that will lead you into the truths of this principle that are relevant to every area of your life—relevant to your well being, your spirit, your soul, your body, your marriage, your relationships, your finances—every single area.

I am going to show you the keys to positioning yourself in God's order of things, which releases His promises in your life. Once this revelation truly hits your spirit, your life will not be the same!

CHAPTER 1

Empowered to Prosper and Succeed

God has good things for you—He *wants* you to be blessed. But what does that really mean? Have you ever thought about it? You've probably heard people say things like "count your blessings," or "I received a wonderful blessing today." But God's desire to bless you goes much deeper than that. The word "blessed" really means to be *empowered to prosper and to succeed*. Before his death, and before the children of Israel took their first steps into the land of promise, Moses was very particular in describing the blessings of God to them.

> All these blessings will come upon you and accompany you if you obey the LORD your God:
>
> You will be blessed in the city and blessed in the country. The fruit of your womb will be blessed, and the crops of your land and the young of your livestock—the calves of your herds and the lambs of your flocks. Your basket and your kneading trough will be blessed. You will be blessed when you come in and blessed when you go out.
>
> The LORD will grant that the enemies who rise up against you will be defeated before you. They will come at you from one direction but flee from you in seven.

The LORD will send a blessing on your barns and on everything you put your hand to. The LORD your God will bless you in the land he is giving you.

The LORD will establish you as his holy people, as he promised you on oath, if you keep the commands of the LORD your God and walk in his ways. Then all the peoples on earth will see that you are called by the name of the LORD, and they will fear you. The LORD will grant you abundant prosperity—in the fruit of your womb, the young of your livestock and the crops of your ground—in the land he swore to your forefathers to give you.

The LORD will open the heavens, the storehouse of his bounty, to send rain on your land in season and to bless all the work of your hands. You will lend to many nations but will borrow from none (Deuteronomy 28:2-13 NIV).

That is quite a list! I want you to notice the fact that essentially every aspect of life is included in that blessing. Everywhere you go, your children, your herds, your flocks, your crops, your barns (in modern terminology that means your business, your bank accounts, your relationships, your mind and your home) will all be blessed and overflowing, and everything you put your hand to will prosper. So, when you hear me or someone else say, "God wants to bless you," remember: He wants to give *you*—His people—the power to prosper and succeed!

I consider John 10:10 to be the mission statement of Jesus' ministry on earth. He said, "The thief cometh not, but for to steal, and to kill, and to destroy: I am come that they might have life, and that they might have it more abundantly." The Amplified version of the Bible reads: "…I came that they may have and enjoy life, and have it in abundance (to the full, till it overflows)."

Peter proclaimed that God has given us "everything we need for life and godliness through our knowledge of him who called us by his own glory and goodness" (2 Peter 1:3 NIV). God is not limited by the economy…He is not limited by a government…and He is certainly not limited by the heathen or the enemy. He is God. Everything you need has already been provided! As Paul said in Ephesians 3:20, "Now unto him that is able to do exceeding abundantly above all that we ask or think, according to the power that worketh in us, unto him be glory in the church by Christ Jesus throughout all ages, world without end."

GOD'S ORDER

With that in mind, I want to begin laying a very simple foundation that will lead you into some deep truths that are relevant to every area of your life—relevant

When the psalmist spoke of God being magnified or en-larged, he was speaking of God fulfilling His covenant. Notice again in Deuteronomy 28:9: "The LORD will establish you as his holy people, as he promised you on oath..." That oath is His covenant, His unfailing, un-changing covenant. Moses goes on to say, "Then all the peoples on earth will see *that you are called by the name of the LORD*, and they will fear you" (v. 10 NIV; emphasis added).

So, right in the middle of God listing the blessings that His people will enjoy if they are obedient and walk in His ways, He tells them that all the nations of the earth will "see that you are called by the name of the LORD." When God's blessings are manifested in our lives, when we are operating with the power He gives us to prosper and succeed, people notice. In fact, it causes God to be magnified, swelled up, enlarged in their eyes. He is our source and our provider, and when our lives reflect the evidence of His blessings, people see that God is indeed good! Whether you are aware of it or not, people are watching your life. You are a living testimony to the saved and unsaved, declaring what you have seen and heard God do for you. Your life is proof of God's goodness and mercy.

Think about a caring, compassionate earthly father who gives his daughter a wonderful gift...her favorite doll, for example. What pride he takes in giving that gift to his daughter, especially when he hears her tiny voice boldly and joyously proclaim to everyone she meets, "My

Daddy gave her to me!"

God is *magnified*—not when we are broke, busted and disgusted—but when we prosper as a result of *trusting* Him. Consider the young woman whose marriage is about to fall apart. It seems that hope is lost, but she maintains her faith, praying and believing God for His provision over her household. Instead of separating, divorcing, and finding herself and her two small children living in a run-down apartment, barely making ends meet, people around her see her working through the difficulties with God's grace. Instead of divorce, they see her and her husband drawing closer and starting to build a stronger relationship than they ever had before. And as a result, those who were watching are drawn closer to the God she serves because she is walking in blessings.

I am not implying that there will never be difficult times or bad things that happen. Bad things do happen to good people. What I am saying is, you can have the peace that passes all understanding even when things are rough. When the enemy comes in one way, he's going to have to flee seven ways. Anything that the enemy steals from you, he must restore it sevenfold. Anything you willingly offer up to the Lord will always come back as a blessing. God has promises for you that cannot fail. So people may see you in a pit, but they will also see God cause you to be triumphant over your circumstances and promoted to a palace! God wants to be magnified and show Himself big in your life.

COVENANT PROSPERITY

One thing we need to do is get a better understanding about the real meaning of prosperity. You see, prosperity is a *wholeness* word. Though it includes finances, in Deuteronomy 28 and throughout the Word, we see that it means so much more. God's prosperity is really about *everything* in your life functioning and operating correctly.

The Bible declares in Psalm 115:14, "The Lord shall increase you more and more, you and your children." No matter what you have been through in your life, God has much greater things in store for you. According to the Word of God, I expect increase to come into your life as He continues to take you from glory, to glory, to glory.

Psalm 5:12 reads, "For thou, Lord, wilt bless the righteous; with favor wilt thou compass him as with a shield." God will hedge you in with *favor*. Do you know what favor is? Favor is undeserved access. God's favor takes you places you could never go on your own. It will take an Esther and make her a queen overnight for "such a time as this." Favor will raise you up out of obscurity into notoriety. Favor will cause Boaz to find you, Ruth. Favor will pull you out of the pit and put you into a palace, Joseph. Favor will turn your famine into a feast. Favor will promote you. It will give you access to places that have been closed off to you. It will do for you what your résumé cannot do for you...what money, a mate, or ministry cannot do for you.

But notice this—with that favor, God will also protect you as with a shield. Like Solomon wrote in Proverbs 10:22, "The blessing of the Lord, it maketh rich, and he addeth no sorrow with it." In the Amplified it reads, "The blessing of the Lord—it makes [truly] rich, and He adds no sorrow with it [neither does toiling increase it]." Not only will you be blessed, you will be protected. Your works and abilities cannot make you blessed. Only the Lord gives you the ability to get wealth—the power to prosper and to succeed.

Why? It is part of His covenant. Taking pleasure in prospering His children has to do with fulfilling His promises. It's not so much that we've been doing what is wrong that nullifies the prosperity of God. We need to understand that we're often not doing enough of what is *right*. I want you to think about that a moment. Partial faith does not open up the promises of God.

The Bible is a book of covenant. In fact, both the Old and New Testaments could be called the Old and New Covenants. A covenant deals with transactions between God and man, or man and his fellow man. It is a legal, binding contract. It is God's law. It is God's order. God is very jealous to keep His covenant. The question is, are we? We cannot expect the multiple blessings of God to manifest in our lives if we are not holding up our end of the covenant. You simply cannot have it your way—like Burger King—and expect to get God's results. You have to do it God's way. Hosea 4:6 declares, "My people perish because of lack of knowledge." What we don't know can destroy us.

TAKE OFF THE LIMITATIONS

My God is an awesome God. My God is an immutable God. My God is the same God that showed up as the fourth man in the fiery furnace with Shadrach, Meshach and Abednego. He's the same God who closed the lion's mouth in Daniel's den. He is the same God who drowned Pharaoh's army in the Red Sea after He parted the waters and ushered His people across upon dry ground. He's the same God who showed up at a widow woman's house during a severe famine and caused her barrel of oil to never fail and her meal to never run out. He's the same God who raised the Shunamite woman up as a great woman and gave her a promise. He is the same God who is the Prince of Peace, and He's the same God who rebuilds the walls of life.

I've heard that Smith Wigglesworth said, "Nothing is impossible with God. All the impossibility lies in us, when we measure God by the limitations of our own understanding." So any time there is less than "life more abundant," it means we are living beneath our covenant privileges—we're living short of God's desire for our lives.

Part of what drives me to preach, to teach, and even to write books comes from seeing that many of God's people are *not* prospering. They are not living the fullness of what God sent His Son as a sacrifice to give to us—abundant life. I see lack either in love, or joy, or finances, or health, or peace of mind, or household and family. I talk to people all the time who love the Lord and serve God faithfully, but they struggle day-to-day, week-to-week, month-to-month—just to survive. I know many folks who live "paycheck to paycheck" fearing that at any moment something could happen that would completely wipe out their finances; people who love God but are emotionally depleted and dysfunctional, stressed out, sick, fearful and all too often defeated.

Why are God's people living with lack—that is, tolerating sicknesses and disease, living with stress and torment—instead of experiencing what God has declared for them? We clearly cannot blame God. Obviously the problem is not on His end. So what is it that *we* might be doing wrong? What is holding us back from living the abundant life Jesus talked about? Why can't we move into the realm that God has already established over our lives?

You must be careful to never minimize the majesty and the greatness of God. He is as big as you allow Him to be. I believe God's question to His people is, "Will you take the limitations off Me? Will you let Me be God? Will you not only learn my ways, but live according to my ways?" When you operate in His principles, you take off the limitations. The God who has prepared the blessing for you is the same God who is preparing you for the blessing!

In the next several chapters I am going to reveal to you a covenant truth, a pattern of provision that God instituted from the beginning—even before the tithe.

I believe what I'm about to share with you will cause revelation to hit your spirit…and your life is going to be transformed!

CHAPTER 2

WHY IS THERE LACK?

I have often said, "You cannot conquer what you don't confront; you cannot confront what you don't identify." Poverty is to be depleted or to be in lack of the things you need. Though most people think of poverty as a lack of finances, it is not limited to that any more than prosperity is just a financial term. To prosper means to have wholeness—spirit, soul, mind and body. While it includes your finances, prosperity is not materialism, it is a wholeness word that means *everything* prospering, everything functioning properly in your life. Poverty is depletion—prosperity is wholeness.

What good is it to have money, and yet be bankrupt in your spirit? As Jesus said, "For what shall it profit a man, if he shall gain the whole world, and lose his own soul?" (Mark 8:36).

> You should have peace...
> You should have joy...
> You should have restoration...
> You should have love with your spouse,
> children and significant relationships...
> You should have a right mind...
> You should have freedom and
> liberation...
> *And* you should have enough resources
> to do everything that God has assigned
> in your life and called you to do. That
> is prosperity. That is wholeness!

As we read in the first chapter, God wants to prosper you. But if God mandates that you prosper, if God mandates that you increase, if God mandates abundance in your life, why do you have lack? (It is one thing to experience a season that is difficult—but "having lack" means you live in that continual state.) Why does anyone in the body of Christ have lack? The problem can't be on the giving end. It must be on the receiving end.

REASONS FOR LACK

If there is a lack of joy, lack of finances, lack of restoration, lack of peace, lack of anything that God has for you, then you must first identify the cause of that lack before you can overcome it. As it is often said, only a fool will expect different results from doing the exact same thing over and over. We are not called to be foolish but wise! There are several reasons the Bible gives for having lack in our lives. I want to cover some of them for you in order to examine the areas of your life that are not "abundant," giving you the tools to make the "adjustments" that are necessary.

The first biblical reason for lack comes from having an unteachable spirit. Proverbs 13:18 says, "Poverty and shame shall be to him that refuseth instruction: but he that regardeth reproof shall be honoured." The New Living Translation puts it this way: "If you ignore criticism, you will end in poverty and disgrace; if you accept criticism, you will be honored." There have been many times I was so grieved and felt deep concern or sorrow for someone who suddenly decided they needed no accountability or teaching. When you stop learning, you stop growing.

We should all be teachable, no matter who we are, no matter what our social status may be, no matter what God has called or appointed any of us to do in our lifetime. We must continually maintain a teachable spirit, ever learning, ever humble before God. "Humble yourselves in the sight of the Lord, and He shall lift you up" (James 4:10). You could study just one scripture all your life and never get the fullness of the revelation of it. There is so much more depth to God and His Word than we have even begun to understand. A great philosopher once stated, "I am the wisest man of all for I have come to understand that I know nothing."

Remember what God told the Israelites: "Today, if you hear his voice, do not harden your hearts as you did at Meribah, as you did that day at Massah in the desert..." (Psalm 95:7-10). God was angry with them for forty years *and* they never entered His rest—His *best*—for them because they were a "stubborn and stiff-necked people." They were unteachable. If you wonder if you have had an unteachable spirit, ask the Lord. Seek the Holy Spirit—He will show you.

The second reason I see for lack in our lives comes from laziness. God's Word tells us that we become new creatures the moment we accept Jesus as our Savior. That does not mean we instantly experience a new environment, new circumstances, new situations or new relationships. There is a walking out and a working out that is our responsibility. We are the ones who have to create and establish a new atmosphere for our lives—an atmosphere that is focused on God and based on the principles of His Word. Faith is what empowers you to obtain all that God has promised you. We become prosperous and successful when we speak God's Word, meditate on it day and night, and live by it (Joshua 1:8). It takes effort to speak, effort to read and effort to study and meditate on God's Word, and effort to do that every day, day in and day out.

The Bible warns against laziness, "Yet a little sleep, a little slumber, a little folding of the hands to sleep: So shall thy poverty come as one that travaileth; and thy want as an armed man" (Proverbs 24:33-34). Anyone who thinks God is going to simply rain His blessings down on you while you sit back and take it easy—you've been deceived. Remember: The devil is a liar! He does not want you blessed, because then you will magnify God to all who watch your life. Laziness will never allow you to experience the fullness of the promises of God. Ecclesiastes 5:3 states, "For a dream cometh through the multitude of business; and a fool's voice is known by multitude of words."

We must live by faith, but we are also to put works with our faith (see James 1:22). We are to act, to move out in that faith. You have to be a *doer* of the Word, not just a hearer. You have to work the Word and resist the forces that come against you and *move* in faith. Just as I shared about Hannah in the first chapter—she would not have conceived by just *believing* she would become pregnant. She had to be intimate with her husband. She had to put "work" with her faith in order to conceive her promise.

This third reason is what I believe affects most of us— ignorance. "My people are destroyed for lack of knowledge" (Hosea 4:6). It doesn't get much clearer than that. Destruction is a sure sign of lack! And notice who is destroyed: My people. People who love God and have a relationship with Him are destroyed because of ignorance, a lack of knowledge, an awareness of information. They are lacking in an abundance of life because of the things they do not know. As Solomon said, "By knowledge shall the chambers be filled with all precious and pleasant riches" (Proverbs 24:4). Perhaps you have heard the saying, "It's what you don't know that is killing you." I have found that you can have a "right heart" and a "wrong head," in which case you will live defeated or deficient in areas.

Another cause for a spirit of lack in our lives comes from oppressing the poor. Proverbs 22:16, 22 says, "He that oppresseth the poor to increase his riches, and he that giveth to the rich, shall surely come to want ... Rob not the poor, because he is poor: neither oppress the afflicted in the gate." Oppressing another person means keeping them down. God warned the Israelites about the poor, saying, "Give generously to [the poor] and do so without a grudging heart; then because of this the

LORD your God will bless you in all your work and in everything you put your hand to. There will always be poor people in the land. Therefore I command you to be openhanded toward your brothers and toward the poor and needy in your land" (Deuteronomy 15:10-11 NIV).

God increases the person who takes care of the poor—the person who is openhanded instead of closed-fisted. It is something He is very serious about, even telling the Israelites not to glean every single grain from their fields or grape from their vines, in order to leave some for the poor to harvest for themselves. The Bible tells us that we are not aware that some strangers may even be angels. What if God set you up for promotion by placing someone in your life that had need, that was poor, and you bypassed that person? Find someone that is in a less fortunate situation than you. Give to them. Giving is not isolated to dollars and cents. It may be food, a hug, education, love or time. Everything in life can be a "seed" to be sown into the life of another person.

Sometimes lack simply comes from misfortune. This is clearly demonstrated in the life of the widow of Zarephath. Her story is found in 1 Kings 17. There was great famine in the land, and she had gone through nearly all of her flour and oil, having only enough left to make a small cake for herself and her son. After that, she anticipated starvation to set in, just as it had for so many others. Bad things can happen to good people. But God sent this little widow an opportunity. She had the option to take that cake for herself, and her son, or to make it for the prophet of God instead. That is a tough place to be. We all want to believe we would easily yield to a difficult decision because we are "so spiritual." The truth is, obedience can be difficult when you are in a "pressure situation." But she obeyed the illogical instruction of the prophet and God blessed her with abundance. The flour and oil did not run out, and her son was even raised from the dead!

The Gospel is the book of Good News, and Romans 8:28 is exactly that: "And we know that all things work together for good to them that love God, to them who are the called according to his purpose." So when the enemy does send in misfortune, look at it like this: "It's not my stumbling block. This is just a temporary thing. It's a stepping stone. God's taking what the enemy meant for bad and turning it around for good." Somehow, some way, there is "good" coming out of misfortune!

Lack can also be a direct result of disobedience.

Deuteronomy 28 is all about the blessings of obedience and the curses of disobedience. I listed the blessings in the first chapter (Deuteronomy 28:2-13). But the curses are just as real:

> If you do not obey the LORD your God and do not carefully follow all his commands and decrees I am giving you today, all these curses will come upon you and overtake you:

You will be cursed in the city and cursed in the country.

Your basket and your kneading trough will be cursed.

The fruit of your womb will be cursed, and the crops of your land, and the calves of your herds and the lambs of your flocks.

You will be cursed when you come in and cursed when you go out.

The LORD will send on you curses, confusion and rebuke in everything you put your hand to, until you are destroyed and come to sudden ruin because of the evil you have done in forsakinghim… (Deuteronomy 28:15-20 NIV).

God does not "curse you," but your direct disobedience brings consequences that can hurt you and others, and potentially be tragic. That is why God declares, "To obey is better than sacrifice" (1 Samuel 15:22).

Withholding will lead to lack in our lives. Solomon's wealth and wisdom were the stuff of legend, even beyond the biblical accounts. If ever there was a man who suffered no lack, it was Solomon. Consider what he meant when he wrote, "One man gives freely, yet gains even more; another withholds unduly, but comes to poverty. A generous man will prosper; he who refreshes others will himself be refreshed. People curse the man who hoards grain, but blessing crowns him who is willing to sell" (Proverbs 11:24-26 NIV). Our God expects us to deal generously with others, trusting Him to provide for our needs.

Part of getting "first things first" is to identify those things in your life that may be holding you back from walking in God's best. Once you can identify the problem, you are empowered to change it. If there is lack in your life, I encourage you to use the "spotlight" of God's Holy Spirit to identify—and conquer—whatever is holding you back.

FAMINE IN THE LAND

Imagine making a living by shepherding a small flock of sheep, and for a little side income, you spend a couple of hours each day skillfully cultivating several fig trees that grow wild on your property. Experience has taught you the essential principles of sowing a seed and—given the right conditions—seeing it produce a crop far beyond what you sowed. You have endured seasons of plenty and times of leanness, times of rain and times of near barrenness, and through it all God has been faithful.

In fact, God has been speaking to you over the years, stirring your heart with an intense burden for His Word and His people. Finally, He speaks again, only this time He sends you from your tiny hometown all the way to northern Israel—to prophesy against the people there, in the hope of turning their hearts back to God.

Of course, the life I am describing is that of the prophet Amos, the so-called slow-of-tongue farmer from Tekoa, just outside of Bethlehem. (Personally, I think his southern accent just sounded peculiar to the folks in northern Israel.) Though he was what most would call a simple farmer, Amos was by no means ignorant, as evidenced by his writings. If his words came slowly, it was most likely because of the tremendous burden on his heart and the weight of the words to be delivered.

After all, though God commanded the humble prophet to tell Israel many hard things, the following words *should* have been the most utterly terrifying. Amos said in Chapter 8, verses 11-12:

> Behold, the days come, saith the Lord
> GOD, that I will send a famine in the
> land, not a famine of bread, nor a thirst
> for water, *but of hearing the words of the*
> *LORD:* And they shall wander from sea
> to sea, and from north even to the east,
> they shall run to and fro to seek the word
> of the LORD, and shall not find it.

Amazingly, Amos' dire prophecy did not have the urgent impact on the people that you might expect. His words came at a time when Israel had a great number of prophets in the land and abundant opportunities for hearing the word of the Lord.

Sounds a little like the world today, doesn't it?

37

How terrifying to think that today, we could be guilty of *hearing* the Word of God to the point that we are numb to it; so much so that we no longer walk in the fullness of His promises, that we no longer follow His principles, that we no longer fear or reverence the Lord!

King Solomon told us that, *"The fear of the LORD is the beginning of knowledge"* (Proverbs 1:7). What happens when there is no understanding, no knowledge of God's Word? The prophet Hosea made God's concern very real when he said, "My people are destroyed for lack of knowledge…" (Hosea 4:6).

DEATH TO ABUNDANCE

I will explain this in more detail in the following chapters, but I want you to begin to see that the lack of knowledge of God's Word brings death to things that should be abundant in your life. It causes you to lean on the arm of the flesh and make decisions from that position more than trusting in God. Wherever there is lack in an area of our lives, we should search our hearts—and His Word—and find out what is missing, or perhaps what we don't know.

What we now know as God's Word—the Bible—was still being recorded in the days of Amos. Imagine not having the Bible we have today. The Bible is our source—God's Word to us. When Jesus was being tempted in the desert to turn the stones into bread, He answered, "It is written: 'Man does not live on bread alone, but on every word that comes from the mouth of God'" (Matthew

4:4 NIV). God's Word cannot fail to operate in our lives when applied appropriately. Yet with all the teaching, prophecy, books, tapes and different versions and colors of the Bible that are available today—people are still perishing for a lack of knowledge of God's Word, and not doing what God has revealed through His Word (see James 1:22).

Are we bored with the Truth? Are we so well fed on God's Word that we have become numb to its principles and precepts? We must heed the word of the prophets of long ago, and set our hearts to knowledge and understanding.

I personally know what it is to live in a place of "lack" for a long time. A lack of love, wholeness, provision, protection, security, peace (just to start the "lack list" that dominated my life). I also know what it is to live in "abundance," to be content in all things with a peace that passes all understanding and to have provision for each season and an inner fortitude to build the life God had masterfully designed for me.

I do not want you to have lack in any area of your life, and I am going to do everything I can to show you the things that God has revealed to me over the past several years that will show you how to live in the fullness of His covenant—the abundant life Jesus spoke of in John 10:10.

Always remember: Abundance is not limited to financial increase. In His parable of the sheep and the good shepherd, Jesus is the one who gives life (as opposed to the thief who kills), and life more abundantly, meaning for sheep: good pasture, safety, health, guidance, etc. Just as lack is not limited to affecting only your finances, likewise, abundance relates to every area of your life.

CHAPTER 3

PROMISES AND PRINCIPLES

D o you want to take hold of these precious promises? Do you desire to live the abundant life that Jesus gave His life to make available to those who believe in Him? It is possible, but we cannot live like the Israelites of long ago, overindulged on the Word of God but having no real knowledge of His patterns, principles and precepts.

> For the LORD giveth wisdom: out of his mouth cometh knowledge and under-standing (Proverbs 2:6).
>
> A scorner seeketh wisdom, and find-eth it not: but knowledge is easy unto him that understandeth." (Proverbs 14:6) The Amplified version of this verse says, "A scoffer seeks Wisdom in vain [for his very attitude blinds and deafens him to it], but knowledge is easy to him who [being teachable] understands (AMP).

According to Proverbs 2:6, *knowledge* comes from the *study* of God's Word. God gives wisdom, but out of His mouth—from studying and understanding His *Word*—we gain knowledge. We cannot fully comprehend the vastness of all God has for those who are His. But God has given us His Word to study, in order to attain the knowledge we need to release God's plan and desire to prosper every area of our lives, as He confirms

His covenant.

God's covenant is His law. With that covenant we have everything we need, every promise of God is ours. As Peter wrote to those in exile after the resurrection of Jesus:

> Grace and peace be multiplied to you *in the knowledge* of God and of Jesus our Lord; Seeing that His divine power has granted to us everything pertaining to life and godliness, *through the true knowledge* of Him who called us by His own glory and excellence. For by these He has granted to us His *precious and magnificent promises*, so that by them you may become partakers of the divine nature, having escaped the corruption that is in the world by lust (2 Peter 1: 2-4 NASB; emphasis added).

The precious and magnificent promises of God allow us to become more like Him, and less like the world. Through Christ, these promises give us everything we need. But without the true knowledge of His Word, many of the promises of God may go unrealized in your life.

We must have a fresh revelation of God's truth. We need to understand His covenant and His principles if we are going to walk in His fullness. We must see through the eyes of God with His perception. God wants to take you from increase to increase (Psalm 115:14). He has good things for you! How it must break God's heart to see His children doing without when He has given us everything we need.

BLINDED EYES

When Nicodemus, a Pharisee and a member of the Jewish ruling council, came privately to speak with the Lord, Jesus told him, "I tell you the truth, no one can *see* the kingdom of God unless he is born again" (John 3:3 NIV; emphasis added). The Bible says except a man be born again, he cannot *see*. The Greek word used there for "see" means "to comprehend, understand and have revelation." The moment an unbeliever accepts Jesus as his or her Lord and Savior, he or she begins to see and begins to understand kingdom things. Someone who is not born again will never be able to see or function in God's ways or His Kingdom.

Nicodemus was shocked by the Lord's statement and didn't understand. Jesus pointed out that Nicodemus was one of Israel's *teachers*, yet he did not understand the kingdom of God. Then Jesus told him, "I tell you the truth, we speak of what we know, and we testify to what we have seen, but still you people do not accept our testimony" (John 3:10-11 NIV).

That's why there is no reason to argue with your unsaved friends and relatives over things like bringing your tithes to the storehouse, forsaking not the assembling together (attending church), keeping the Commandments of God or honoring your relationship with Him through obedience to His Word. They don't "get it." You can tell them what you have seen and know, but they will not understand why you come to church three times a week, pray, fast, tithe or stay faithful to the Lord with no "apparent" reward—at least in their eyes.

Sadly, they cannot understand it because their eyes have not been opened. "The god of this age has blinded the minds of unbelievers, so that they cannot see the light of the gospel of the glory of Christ, who is the image of God" (2 Corinthians 4:4 NIV). Unless a person is born again, they cannot comprehend, see or have revelation of the way God does things or "His system of operation."

The ways of the world are quite different from the ways of God. For example, the world says to "get, take, hoard," but God says we are to give away in order to receive. Look at what Jesus told the rich young ruler who wanted to know what good deed he needed to do to possess eternal life. Jesus told him to follow the commandments.

> The young man said, "I have observed all these from my youth; what still do I lack?"
>
> Jesus answered him, "If you would be perfect [that is, have that spiritual maturity which accompanies self-sacrificing character], go and sell what you have and

give to the poor, and you will have riches in heaven; and come, be My disciple."

But when the young man heard this, he went away sad (grieved and in much distress), for he had great possessions.

And Jesus said to His disciples, "Truly I say to you, it will be difficult for a rich man to get into the kingdom of heaven" (Matthew 19:20-23 AMP).

I used the Amplified translation of this well-known story to pull some of the deeper meaning out of the text. Notice the "self-sacrificing character" is related to "perfection" in the kingdom of God. The world's ways are typically to step on somebody to get to the top, to sleep with somebody to make your way to the top, to manipulate your way to the top. On the contrary, God says you've got to "crucify your flesh" and die to your way of doing things in order to live. God's ways are not man's ways. They're often absolute opposites.

Jesus emphasized how difficult it is for a "rich man" to enter the Kingdom of Heaven (Matthew 19:23-24). Let me make it clear: God does not have a problem with you being "rich." In fact He speaks more about money than almost anything in the New Testament. His first promise to Abraham—our father of faith—was to make him wealthy (rich). That promise was inherited by all New Testament believers according to Galatians 3:29. It is in effect for you today! When Jesus declared the difficulty for a "rich" man to enter, He was saying in essence…"How hard will it be for a man who has done it his way to now change, turn direction and do things God's way."

As I mentioned, being born again is just the beginning. You cannot sit around lazily expecting all God's blessings to overtake you. A good way to explain this is found in Jesus' teaching in John 8:31-32:

> Then said Jesus to those Jews which be-
> lieved on him, "If ye continue in my
> word, then are ye my disciples indeed;
> And ye shall know the truth, and the
> truth shall make you free."

The word "continue" in the Greek means to stay, abide, dwell, endure, remain. And if we look up "disciples" in the original text, it means a learner or a pupil. And of course "free" in the Greek means to liberate, deliver, make free. Reading this same passage in the Amplified brings even more clarity: "So Jesus said to those Jews who had believed in Him, 'If you abide in My word [hold fast to My teachings and live in accordance with them], you are truly My disciples. And you will know the Truth, and the Truth will set you free.'"

As believers, it is the truth that you *know*, the truth that you have revelation of that makes you free, liberated, delivered. Knowledge comes from the study of God's Word. These verses make it clear why we are to get the

Word in our hearts and minds and stand on the Word at all times. You don't walk with God according to what you *feel*. You walk by what you *know*. Eve knew she was forbidden to eat of the tree in the center of the garden, but the enemy's cunning convinced her to act on her feelings instead of on her knowledge—and that didn't work out very well. As David said, "My eyes anticipate the night watches and I am awake before the cry of the watchman, that I may meditate on Your word" (Psalm 119:148 AMP).

Remember what I noted earlier—you are motivated to move and act by the revelation of truth. Acting in faith on that revelation is what releases the promises of God in your life. It is the truth or Word that you know that will bring the promises of God in your life. The Word is your covenant, your legal binding contract. All privileges are released through believing and receiving the Word.

CARNAL VS. SPIRITUAL MIND

Prosperity has to do with much more than just your finances. As the disciple John wrote to his dear friend Gaius, and all who would read the letter after him: "Beloved, I wish above all things that thou mayest prosper and be in health, even as thy soul prospereth" (3 John 1:2). Now, understanding that your soul is your mind, your will and your emotions, it is easy to see how your outward life is a reflection of the condition of your soul. So if your soul—mind, will, emotions—is prospering, then the other areas of your life should prosper in like manner.

> Do not conform any longer to the
> pattern of this world, but be transformed
> by the renewing of your mind. Then you
> will be able to test and approve what
> God's will is—his good, pleasing and
> perfect will. For by the grace given me I
> say to every one of you: Do not think of
> yourself more highly than you ought,
> but rather think of yourself with sober
> judgment, in accordance with the
> measure of faith God has given you
> (Romans 12:2-3 NIV).

Your life is transformed as your mind is renewed or
"renovated." To renovate means to take away the old and
put in the new.

I will refer to Deuteronomy 8, verses 17 and 18
frequently throughout this book because it is founda-
tional to the principle of first fruits. It says, "And thou
say in thine heart, My power and the might of mine hand
hath gotten me this wealth. But thou shalt remember the
Lord thy God: for it is he that giveth thee power to get
wealth, that he may establish his covenant which he sware
unto thy fathers, as it is this day." Paul certainly understood these words of God when he warned believers not
to "think of yourself more highly than you ought, but
rather think of yourself with sober judgment" (Romans

12:3 NIV).

The mind of the flesh says, "I've done all this with my abilities," but the mind of God acknowledges that He is the one who gives you the ability to get wealth. I am talking about carnal mindedness vs. spiritual mindedness here—which is a crucial point to understand. As Paul warned, "To be carnally minded is death; but to be spiritually minded is life and peace. Because the carnal mind is enmity against God: for it is not subject to the law of God, neither indeed can be. So then they that are in the flesh cannot please God" (Romans 8:6-8).

If you are walking in the flesh, you are not walking by faith; "For they that are after the flesh do mind the things of the flesh; but they that are after the Spirit the things of the Spirit" (Romans 8:5). Without faith, it is impossible to please God. Further, a carnal, fleshly mind brings death. I don't know about you, but these are very *sobering* words!

Let's break it down even further. I would say, based on these verses of scripture, that anything that is dying in your life can be traced back to a decision made with a carnal mind.

On the contrary, everything that has abundance, life and peace, you can trace back to a decision made with a spiritual mind. Look at the fruit of your life. What do you see? Are your finances in alignment with God's word? Are your relationships in alignment with God's word? Is your physical body in alignment with God's word? If you are to prosper as your soul prospers, what condition is your soul in?

From my own life experiences, I could take you through almost every emotional, psychological, physical, or natural disaster a person could walk through. For many years death was produced in my life from carnal mindedness. When I was just five years old, my father, my hero, committed suicide. Not understanding the reasons for his actions, my young mind decided it must have been because I wasn't good enough. Our fragile family soon experienced financial devastation after the death of my father. A year later, a cycle of sexual abuse began to twist my life into even deeper places of confusion and shame. Those carnal thoughts sent me into a tailspin of seeking to please others and even manipulating to get what I wanted throughout my childhood and teenage years.

But when I surrendered, accepting Christ as my Savior, and was born again, my carnal mind that I'd grown so used to serving began a process of transformation. My mind began to be renewed on the Word of God. Even when I fell terribly ill in the mid-90's and the doctors examining me said my lungs were only operating at a fraction of the normal percentage, the mind of the Spirit was my comfort. They gave me a bleak prognosis with no hope, but I believed the Word of God for my healing. Abiding in the Word of God, doing things God's way, not only transformed my mind, but also gave me revelation to walk in the provision of healing that God had already made for my life.

God's provision for you is a complete package. Paul said, "Set your minds on things above, not on earthly things. For you died, and your life is now hidden with Christ in God" (Colossians 3:2-3 NIV). So if you find death in an area of your life, it could be because there was a decision made somewhere with the carnal mind. If you find life, there's a decision made somewhere with the spiritual mind. Now, let me show you something.

AGREEMENT WITH GOD

I mentioned Hebrews 11:6 before: "But without faith it is impossible to please him: for he that cometh to God must believe that he is, and that he is a rewarder of them that diligently seek him." Now, it is important to understand "please Him." It has nothing to do with getting God to like us or approve of us. It is wrong to think, "God, am I making you happy? Lord, do you approve of me? If I can work enough faith, will you approve of me?"

The Greek word for "please" means to come into alignment or to come into agreement with God. In other words, without the Word working in your life, it is impossible for you to come into alignment or think like God, see like God, act like God, and do like God. You cannot separate God from His Word. He makes Himself synonymous or "One" with the Word. John 1:1 says, "In the beginning was the Word, and the Word was with God, and the Word was God" (NIV). So without faith, it's impossible for me to line up with the Word. Faith is the Word and the Word is faith. That is why the Bible says God's people perish for lack of knowledge...lack of knowledge of the Word...lack of having the Word deep in their spirits...lack of acting on that Word. When we are not in alignment with God, when our minds are not renewed on His Word, there is death.

I want to see the prophetic promises of the Word of God manifested in your life. I want to position you for abundant life! It is time to stop living with lack, with death, and start living as God desires. God is no respecter of persons. He does not want to bless one person and leave someone else behind. He wants everybody corporately to manifest the promise that He has for them.

That is why I want to do everything I can to help you get the principle of First Fruits deep into your spirit. My husband, Randy, and I have lived by this principle since God began to reveal it in our lives years ago, and God's blessings in our lives have truly been abundant. The funny thing is—I didn't even know what the principle was when God began to teach me about first fruits. I simply had a willing heart to obey His "voice."

CHAPTER 4

"Give it All"

When David was only a shepherd of his father's sheep, he was promised a kingdom. When he was still hiding and running for his life from King Saul, he was promised victory. It is little wonder how he could praise God with words like, "My eyes stay open through the watches of the night, that I may meditate on your promises" (Psalm 119:148 NIV). David knew how to keep the Main Thing, the main thing. Even when he was in the desert of Judah, with no place to lay his head, no food and no water, his heart cried out in thirst for God above all else (see Psalm 63:1).

God's promises are not manifested on the basis of any good works you or I have done, or can do. The principle of the first fruits offering is not about *winning* God's favor, but about *releasing* it—acting in faith, which positions you to see those promises manifest in your life. It is your faith in Him that releases God's promises to you. Faith is what empowers you to obtain all that God has promised you. And it was in faith that I responded to the first promptings of the Holy Spirit to give a first fruits offering.

I am still amazed by the way God began to reveal this powerful principle in my life. It wasn't through a sudden and divine "impartation" of revelation. He led me into the knowledge of first fruits step by step as I responded in faith and obedience. I believe the Lord wanted me to truly get an understanding of first fruits on a practical level, so He actually prompted Randy and me to give first fruits before we fully realized what we were doing.

D.C. TO TAMPA

Randy and I married after dating for about three years. During that time, we had served on staff at National Church of God with Dr. T.L. Lowery in Washington, D.C. Randy had served in different capacities in different seasons, and was their associate pastor and evangelism director at one point. I was the children's pastor and headed up the bus ministry to the inner city, which is where my heart for that vital ministry started. It has always been a huge part of my life and who I am.

Just prior to our wedding, Randy was reading through a Christian magazine when something startled him. On the very back cover was a tiny line that read, "Tampa, Florida." I don't even remember what it related to now, but when he noticed it, he said those two words seemed to stand out almost three dimensionally. Realizing God was confirming something in his spirit, Randy called me. He said, "Paula, God just showed me that we are to go to Tampa, Florida."

To be honest with you—I laughed. Not only that, I said something to the effect of "Yeah, sure," and hung-up the phone! I really did. I couldn't imagine moving, and I thought he had to be joking because our family, our security, our finances, everything was there in D.C. Randy had several businesses and things were going very well. We were very comfortable.

When we told our pastor, Dr. Lowery's initial response was to offer us other ministry opportunities within the covering of the church. He came up with

57

several alternatives to our leaving, but then he began to fast and pray. During that time, God confirmed to him, as well, that we were to go to Tampa. He released us with his blessing, covered us spiritually, and remains our pastor to this day.

We have lived with the mentality that, if something is not enough to be your harvest, it's your seed. So we sowed most of our things by giving them away to anyone who could use them. We sold other things so we could leave D.C with as little debt as possible. With $1200, a U-haul truck, a big God and big promises, we headed south for Florida.

God began right away to do a deeper work in our hearts. After driving for two days, we did not feel terribly picky about where we stayed that first night, nor did we have the money for a luxury hotel. Exhausted, we found a little motel, got a room and went right to bed. The next morning we discovered the little motel was the type of place that offered not only nightly, but *hourly* rates as well. Needless to say, we found different lodging right away.

"NOW IS THE TIME"

Soon after we arrived, Randy and I began working as youth pastors at a local church. Even though we dropped from a significant and substantial income to only making about $18,000 a year, we were supernaturally sustained throughout that season. After the first year, the church went through a leadership change, and we were released into what God had begun to prepare our hearts for. We went on a 21-day fast, and God began to clearly show us "now is the time."

We started reaching out to the indigent by feeding the hungry, clothing those in need, and reaching out to the community with the Word and practical help. Some of the people we worked with had begun to call us their pastors. Through God's favor, a man gave us use of a small office space on Manhattan Avenue in Tampa. It was very tiny, but it was a start. We wallpapered and painted and got it set up for Bible studies and outreach.

Just after getting our little storefront office/church arranged, I received an unusual request. I was invited to speak about inner city outreach by a Greek Orthodox Church in the area. It was a wonderful opportunity, that was very humbling, to consider me to actually "speak." We saw God do wonderful things and many precious people in that church who had a heart for the inner cities got some practical insight on effective outreach.

Now, I said we were supernaturally sustained—and we were—but that didn't mean we had any "extra." Though we had started a small ministry, we weren't taking any income from it for ourselves, so we had very little on which to live. When I was given a $200 honorarium for speaking at the Greek Orthodox Church that night, I was ecstatic. It was a tremendous blessing. As I like to put it, I got a "vision" that we were finally going to have hamburger for our "Helper" and cheese for our "Macaroni." At that time, being given $200 was like

having $2 million.

One evening, Randy and I decided to attend a service at a local church in Tampa to be refreshed and receive the Word. That same night they had a guest speaker. I still had the $200 check in my purse. At one point during his message, the guest speaker said, "God is speaking to someone here tonight to give it all." I didn't respond. I just put my head down thinking that $200 *was* our all, and that surely this moment shall pass. Then he said it again. It was as if God was standing right in front of me saying, "What are you going to do?"

All is *all*...whether you are speaking of $200 or $2 million. Letting go of it is still a sacrifice. But I looked at my husband, and he nodded his head in agreement. So I gave that sacrificial seed gift of $200 that night, trusting God to sustain and bless us. I have to admit, as Randy and I left the service that night, I jokingly said, "There goes our cheese for our macaroni...man, they got us." We were kidding around about it, but I am sure my mind was struggling with what we had just done. Sometimes it is hard not to waiver a little between faith and doubt, but I had learned to be obedient and soft-hearted when the Lord spoke to my heart, so I comforted myself that I had indeed given in faith.

A 5′ 2″ MESSENGER

The next day, Randy and I were at our little office/church when the door opened suddenly. I looked up to see a lady with red hair, standing at about 5'2" tall, approaching me. She walked with purpose, and a little bit of an attitude. I wasn't sure what to expect. She walked directly up to Randy and me, handed us an envelope and said, "God kept me up all night last night. Here…take it." She abruptly turned and walked out the same way she came in. We opened the envelope. Inside was a check for $10,000. I could hardly believe it! To be handed that amount of money the day after "giving it all" with that $200 offering was amazing. Of course, my faith was "leaping" then…I knew we had heard from God. But it didn't stop there.

About two hours later, while we were still astounded and in deep gratitude to the Lord over that incredible gift from Him…the same lady came back *again*. With the same attitude with which she delivered the first gift, she marched right up to us with another envelope and said, "Here. God said to give it *all*," and with that, she turned and marched right back out of the door. That envelope contained a check for $5000! With that $15,000 offering we rented the auditorium of a nearby high school, and began the first services of what is now known as Without Walls International Church, and has become one of the largest churches in the nation, reaching many lives for the glory of God.

When we left D.C., we gave just about everything we had. When we started the ministry, we gave our all. What I didn't realize was, God had taught me the power in the principle of first fruiting, before I even fully realized what we were doing. I simply knew to be obedient to what He was saying to my heart, and if He said give it all, I obeyed, even though it wasn't easy. In the next few chapters I am going to teach you the important principals of how God sees things, His order and the law of firsts. You will see how, without me fully comprehending the law, the Word still worked in my life when activated.

THE FIRST FRUITS OF A NEW SEASON

Shortly after I heard the gospel for the first time and dedicated my life to God, I held up the Bible and declared, "The answers to life are in here–reveal to me Who You are, and who I am. Reveal to me 'life answers'." For two years, with a passionate hunger and insatiable thirst for the Word of God, I studied day and night. During that process, God imparted a vision in my spirit. In that vision there were masses of people as far as I could see. Every time I opened my mouth, there was a manifestation of the presence of God. When I shut my mouth, people would fall off a cliff into darkness. With that, God clearly impressed in my spirit that He had called me to preach the gospel. He showed me that a day would come when every time I opened my mouth, nations would be changed. I knew God wanted to use me to preach to the far reaches of the earth. I was not about to give up on that vision—and He didn't either. But even though I knew the vision was from God, I also knew I had to wait to see it come to pass in His timing and in His way. Though I did not know how, I knew in my heart that He was going to amplify my voice one day.

What an awesome privilege and pleasure to serve God. When I told my pastor of this vision, he put a broom in my hand and assigned me to clean the church! I was ecstatic! A journey of servanthood began that would lead to seeing nations glorifying God. This process continued for many years and still continues today.

Several years after we started Without Walls, I was in Hawaii teaching and training about outreach, and God stirred my heart always with this vision at the forefront. I knew He was telling me, "Now is the time to launch TV ministry." What is funny about that is, there was nothing external or internal that would make someone say, "TV ministry is a natural fit for Paula." Anyone who worked with me back in those days knows how many times we had to retake me just trying to say "God bless you" in front of a camera. I was horrible. I had no natural ability. No confidence. No resource or training to pull from. I had nothing but a rhema word from God that said it would be so.

My first step in preparing to embrace this new season was to discuss it with my husband. I said, "Randy, God has spoken to my spirit that it is time to launch TV ministry." He thought for a moment and answered, "Paula, I completely support you emotionally and spiritually, but our plate is full with all that we are doing with the church." Without Walls had grown so fast there was just no way to take on another big expense or project at that time. But he said, "If this is God, you go for it."

Soon after that conversation, we were attending a

large ministry conference in Texas. The ministry time took a somewhat unusual turn one evening. I'd never seen the leader of the conference do what he did that night under the prompting of the Holy Spirit. Near the end of the service, he began to receive an offering. But it was more like a divine move of God, an act of true worship. There was a marvelous atmosphere in the place. In his directions for the offering, he said God was speaking to some to give $25,000, some to give $15,000, and so on, all the way down to $500, $100 and $50. It was very holy.

Now, since my husband and I are in covenant with this man of God, we sow regularly into his ministry. During the offering, I felt God prompting me to "give it all" in a $25,000 gift. So I began to think of the large gifts we had already given, and in my own mind worked it out that if I gave $5000 that night, combined with other offerings we had sown previously, that would make the $25,000. You know how you justify things in your mind for God, right? But that wasn't what God meant.

Randy and I have always had something we call "he money," and "she money." It's another way of saying, yours…mine…and ours. We have finances with which we run our family, and then some that he saves and does what he desires with, and some that I save and do what I desire with. I had been saving for quite a while and had about $19,000 of "she money" at the time.

As people began to make their way to the front to give, the various designations of givers were gathering at

64

the front into groups. So, leaning on my own under-standing and justification, I made my way toward the group of people giving $5000. I was nearly overwhelmed as I walked toward them. I literally sensed the feeling that my calling, the vision God had given me and said, "It is time," was suddenly beginning to mutate and become crippled. God was allowing me to see how my disobedience was causing death to the vision and call of God on my life. It literally jolted me, and I sensed the Lord say, "I asked you to give it all."

I quickly turned and went back to where Randy was sitting. I said, "Honey, God said give it all. I really need to borrow some of your 'he money' so that I can give the $25,000 offering." He agreed and I brought that offering to the front, and gave it as a true sacrifice, as a true first fruits offering, a giving of it all unto the Lord, in obedience to Him. The next day I received a phone call, and within days an international media ministry now known as Paula White Ministries was launched.

Doors just began to open for us over the next five years. God's favor allowed us to develop in that short period of time what would normally take 20 years to do. I didn't know you were supposed to have a million dollars in the bank when you started a TV ministry. We started it with nothing but a promise from God, one camera, some rent-to-own furniture, one secretary that typed about 23 words per minute, six rotary-dial phones and one computer!

In the natural, there was no way of launching or

surviving in that arena. But God's favor makes a way. And His favor was unleashed in abundance because of our willingness to obey and trust Him and to actively demonstrate that trust by giving first fruits. In hind site, I now clearly see the foundation for every promise God had shown us as part of His purpose in our lives and calling, was built from first fruits.

By the time we were launching the media ministry, we were becoming more familiar with first fruits, but only on a limited basis. For example, we had participated by giving a month of our income at the first of the year, in anticipation of God blessing the rest. But God had given me a greater hunger to really 'excavate' the roots of this principle in order to teach the Body of Christ.

I have always had a hunger for knowledge of the Word, and it wasn't long before I was studying everything I could about this principle. When I began to get the revelation of this, I said, "God, your people need this word!"

I am passionate about seeing people released from bondage and lack to walk in the fullness of what God has given—those precious and magnificent promises available through our true knowledge of Him. Remember: knowledge comes from studying the Word. Then comes revelation, and that is what motivates us to move in faith! Again, we do not have lack because of a provision shortage, but because of a revelation shortage. Now, let me take you deeper in what was revealed to me.

CHAPTER 5

UNDERSTANDING
THE PRINCIPLE

The Hebrew word for first fruits, *bikkurim*, means "a promise to come," and shares the same root word, *bekhor*, as the word meaning "firstborn." Yom HaBikkurim, the Jewish festival celebrating the Feast of First Fruits, is one of the most mentioned feasts in the Bible, second only to Passover.

In ancient days, the process of gathering the first fruits of the crops involved painstaking preparations. Each family among the Israelites had to carefully watch for the first budding fruits or grains. Once spotted, they would designate it as the first by tying a piece of red yarn around the branch, limb or vine.

As the crops matured and were harvested, those first fruits were brought into the Temple and presented to the High Priest according to God's pattern. The Priest would accept the offering from each household, and lift it in a wave offering high above his head, presenting it to the God of Israel in thanksgiving and recognition of His continued provision and blessing. Once the offering of the first fruits had been made, the people were free to enjoy the rest of the harvest, because the first had sanctified the rest.

DEVOTED TO THE LORD

The principal of first fruits was not limited to vegetation. It is found throughout the Word, and deals with all "first things." As I studied about the process of marking the first of the crops, I remembered the story of Tamar, found in Genesis, chapter 38. She was in labor with

Judah's twin sons, and it must have been a painful ordeal. The story goes, "As she was giving birth, one of [the twins] put out his hand; so the midwife took a scarlet thread and tied it on his wrist and said, 'This one came out first'" (Genesis 38:28 NIV). However, the little guy who would come to be named Zerah drew his hand back in, and his brother, named Perez, was actually born first. What an ordeal! But it was apparently not uncommon to even mark the first born of twins in such a manner.

Notice the instructions God gave to Moses as He prepared the Israelites to be led out of slavery in Egypt:

> And it shall be when the LORD shall bring thee into the land of the Canaanites, as he sware unto thee and to thy fathers, and shall give it thee, That thou shalt set apart unto the LORD all that openeth the matrix, and every firstling that cometh of a beast which thou hast; the males shall be the LORD's. And every firstling of an ass thou shalt redeem with a lamb; and if thou wilt not redeem it, then thou shalt break his neck: and all the firstborn of man among thy children shalt thou redeem (Exodus 13:11-13).

By now you've probably noticed that I like to take a look at some scriptures in the Amplified version of the Bible as well, just to get a little better insight. It reads:

"You shall set apart to the Lord all that first opens the womb. All the firstlings of your livestock that are males shall be the Lord's. Every firstborn of a donkey you shall redeem by [substituting for it] a lamb, or if you will not redeem it, then you shall break its neck; and every firstborn among your sons shall you redeem." (Exodus 13:11-13 AMP)

God claims the right to every *first*—the first of the crops, every firstborn male of herds and flocks, every first-born male child. Every *first* is to be devoted to God through His covenant. Any time something is called a first thing, a first fruit, a devoted thing, it belongs to God. And, if it is devoted to Him, the Word of God declares that it is better to *destroy* it than to use it for yourself. I will go into more detail on this in the next chapter.

In Exodus 22:29, God instructs Israel again saying, "Thou shalt not delay to offer the first of thy ripe fruits, and of thy liquors: the firstborn of thy sons shalt thou give unto me." The Amplified reads, "You shall not delay to bring to Me from the fullness [of your harvested grain] and the outflow [of your grape juice and olive oil]; give Me the firstborn of your sons [or redeem them]."

Even in the midst of rebuilding their destroyed city, Nehemiah kept to this pattern, and Jerusalem was protected as a result:

...and that they might bring the first
fruits of our ground and the first fruits
of all the fruit of every tree to the house
of the LORD annually, and bring to the
house of our God the firstborn of our
sons and of our cattle, and the firstborn
of our herds and our flocks as it is written
in the law, for the priests who are minis-
tering in the house of our God. We will
also bring the first of our dough, our
contributions, the fruit of every tree, the
new wine and the oil to the priests at the
chambers of the house of our God...
(Nehemiah 10:35-37 NASB).

In Leviticus 27:28-29, God again explained the
instructions for first fruits: "But nothing that a man owns
and devotes to the Lord—whether man or animal or
family or land—may be sold or redeemed; everything so
devoted is most holy to the Lord" (NIV).

FIRST THINGS FIRST

Jesus is the fulfillment of the Old Covenant practice
of obeying this mandate. Thankfully, we no longer
sacrifice the firstlings of our sheep or cattle at a Temple;
nor are we required to redeem our firstborn sons with
gold. Jesus paid for all redemption through His death,
burial and resurrection, giving us a New Covenant
"founded on better promises" (Hebrews 8:6 NIV).

However, the principle of *first things* still remains. God does not change in His character or principals. He is the same yesterday, today and forevermore (see Hebrews 13:8).

God still considers first things to be holy and devoted to Him, but today first fruits has to do with the practice of *keeping the main thing—the main thing*, and God IS the main thing! First fruits means the first in place, order and rank; the beginning, chief or principle thing. God says first things belong to Him in order to establish redeeming covenant with everything that comes after. In God's pattern, whatever is first establishes the rest. The first is the root, from which the rest is determined. Therefore it is better to destroy your first fruits than to use any of it for your own personal gain.

We looked at Exodus 13:12-13 earlier, when God told the Israelites to set apart all of the first-born that opened the womb. But look at what it says in verse 14 (AMP):

> And when, in time to come, your son asks you, "What does this mean?" You shall say to him, "By strength of hand the Lord brought us out from Egypt, from the house of bondage and bondmen."

What were they to remember? What was supposed to be transferred from generation to generation? The

72

knowledge—the acknowledgement—that it was not by their *own strength* that they were led from the land of slavery to the land of promise, but that it was the strength of God's hand. It was to be remembered among the Israelites for all generations that God had been their deliverer and provider. And the mandated offering of first things was established as a reminder for generations to come.

That is why Deuteronomy 8:17-18, though it doesn't seem to speak of first fruits, is so key to unlocking the revelation of this principle. Notice what Joshua says as he begins addressing the Israelites in Deuteronomy 8 verse 1 in the New American Standard Bible:

> All the commandments that I am com-
> manding you today you shall be careful
> to do, that you may live and multiply,
> and go in and possess the land which the
> LORD swore to give to your forefathers.

And in verse 11,

> Beware that you do not forget the
> LORD your God by not keeping His
> commandments and His ordinances and
> His statutes which I am commanding
> you today.

Just as we read in the opening chapter of God's

promises to bless His people, the promise of the blessing
was based on the principle of obedience. God instituted
the principle of first fruits as a means to *remember*.

> Otherwise, you may say in your heart,
> "My power and the strength of my hand
> made me this wealth."
> *But you shall remember the LORD*
> *your God*, for it is He who is giving
> you power to make wealth, that He
> may confirm His covenant which He
> swore to your fathers, as it is this day
> (Deuteronomy 8:17-18 NASB; empha-
> sis added).

THE KEY IS IN *REMEMBERING*

It is so easy to pass over seemingly insignificant portions of scripture simply because we are familiar with
what certain words mean in our own language. That is
why I say again that the greatest reason for lack in the
body of Christ can be traced back to ignorance. Not that
we are ignorant people, but that we are often ignorant,
without knowledge, without study of the deeper things
of God.

You see, we can look right over the term "remember" in Deuteronomy 8:18, because we all know that "to
remember" means to recall, to be mindful of, to retain an
idea or to commemorate someone or something. Often,
the Hebrew word translated "remember" does mean

that. But in this and several other places, it means something more.

In this verse, the Hebrew word is "zakar." "Thou shalt "zakar" the Lord your God…" Zakar means "properly remembered as a male of man or animal, as being the most noteworthy; to mark as to be recognized as male."

Wait a minute…We've just read how the Israelites marked the first fruits of harvest. We also see how God commanded them to devote the first of their flocks and herds, and even their first-born sons to Him as a first fruits offering—to *remember* that it was God who led them out of captivity, that it is God that gives them the ability to get wealth. Now we see God using the word "zakar," which means to properly mark as male…of Himself.

What did the process of marking the first-born male relate to? It relates to the principle of first fruits. Remember, the Hebrew root for first fruits is *bikkurim*, the same as the root for firstborn. So, we could read that scripture in a more literal translation to say,

> But thou shalt *[first fruits]* the LORD
> thy God: for it is he that giveth thee
> power to get wealth…

It is not our ability; it is God's. When we "remember" Him properly, by placing Him as the first and foremost through the offering of first fruits, we are acknowledging that it is God who gives us the ability to prosper and succeed. In other words, when we "first fruit" the Lord, He gives us the ability to get wealth. In this way, the principle of first fruits operating in our lives is the key to walking in the fullness of the promises of God. When we do not violate the principles...then we can claim the promises!

PLACE OF ABUNDANCE

We must recognize that it is not our feeble, limited abilities that release the promises of God. It is not our getting up and driving to work every day that provides the paycheck at the end of the week. No, it is God who blesses us. It is God who gives us the ability, the power, the anointing to get wealth.

Once again I want to remind you that wealth is not limited to your income. Wealth has to do with your whole being, it means nothing missing, nothing broken, nothing out of order (first things first). It means having the blessings that God lists in Deuteronomy 28:2-13 made manifest in your life: peace on all sides, protection, provision, healing, restoration, everything you can imagine. As the psalmist wrote in Psalm 66:12, "We went through fire and water, but you brought us to a place of abundance."

Yes, God wants to bless you, and those abundant blessings are predicated by keeping Him first in your life, a principle God established for the generations through the giving of the first fruits offering. And we see in

Deuteronomy 28:9, as well as in Deuteronomy 8:18, it is through His blessings that He establishes His covenant, causing others to see that the Lord is God!

DIFFERENT FROM THE TITHE

Paul prayed for the Ephesians saying, "I pray also that the eyes of your heart may be enlightened in order that you may know the hope to which he has called you, the riches of his glorious inheritance in the saints, and his incomparably great power for us who believe" (Ephesians 1:18-19 NIV). That is also my prayer for you as you read this book. I want the revelation of the principle of first fruits to go deep into your spirit to motivate you to move out in faith. The only way you will walk in your inheritance is to do so through revelation.

I am burdened when the children of God are living frustrated. I am burdened by God's people merely pleading His promises while unknowingly violating His principles and never seeing God's blessings manifested. I'm tired of God's people being broke, busted and disgusted. I've said it before, and I will keep saying it—I don't believe it is so much that we are doing something *wrong* as it is we are not doing enough of what is right, because we don't have a provision problem—we have a revelation problem. I want you to live in all that Christ died for you to inherit.

Many believe that the tithe, our giving of a tenth of our increase, is the same as first fruits. But the Bible references first fruits, firstlings, or devoted things 32 times, and mentions the tithe 32 times. However, Genesis chapter 4, is the first time that God talks about first fruits, or firstlings, with Cain and Abel. The first time we see the tithe mentioned is in Genesis, chapter 14:18-20, when Abraham tithed to Melchizedek.

Notice in Proverbs 3:10, they are mentioned as two different things: "Honor the Lord with thy first fruits and all thine increase." First fruits is the whole of the first. The tithe refers to the first tenth of the increase. It comes after first fruits. We have often been misled to not understand first fruits, and therefore, we have not walked in the wealthy place that God has for us.

First fruits is not the same as the tithe. First fruits is a principle of keeping first things first; of recognizing, remembering God as the one who gives you the ability to get wealth. First fruits relates to dedicated, devoted, "first" things. Devoted things and dedicated things have the exact same meaning: the irrevocable giving over to the Lord. Deuteronomy 26 gives a distinct delineation between the two offerings.

SEEK YE FIRST

God is very serious about things being in order in our lives. That is why it is so crucial that we understand this principle of *first things first*. When you do not put first things first, everything in your life is out of order. On the other hand, when you do put first things first, everything in your life falls into place. Just as God promised—when we are faithful to follow His commandments, we will be blessed.

God is not a god of confusion. The Greek term for confusion means *disorder*. Notice what James said, "For where you have envy and selfish ambition, there you find disorder and every evil practice" (James 3:16 NIV). Strife means a division, a faction, a pulling away. Where there is division there is confusion—disorder—which opens the door for every evil work and every evil spirit. The reason some of us are fighting such demonic spirits is because we have had disorder in our lives. Where is the wholeness? Where is the wealth? Where is that sense of everything working properly and in order? Remember, God is a god of order.

Well, when we apply the principle of first fruits—first things first—in our lives, we begin to see that all firsts should be given to the Lord: the first part of the day, the first day of the week (Sabbath), the first month of the year, and the first of our harvest–be it the wages for the first hour, the first day, the first week or month.

God tells us to "Remember the sabbath day, to keep it holy" (Exodus 20:8 NASB). We also find the term "zakar" used here for "remember" the Sabbath. The Sabbath is the first of your week. It is what sets the tone for how the rest of your week will go. We are to "first fruit" the Sabbath, to mark it as devoted to the Lord, for Him, not for our own use. We all lead busy lives, but the Sabbath is to be set apart as holy. It is not a shopping day or a workday, nor is it a day for doing your own thing. It is a day for acknowledging the Lord, meditating on His

Word, and rest.

Remember, knowledge comes from studying the Word. Knowledge is often what we lack, yet we have been given a designated day for meditating on God and His Word. We need to ask ourselves…what are we doing with it?

Similarly, what you do first thing in the morning sets the course for the rest of the day. When you wake up say, "Good morning Holy Spirit, I bless you and praise you today, and devote this day to you." Get your day started after you have worshipped and heard from the Lord. God knows you have need of many things, many tasks and things to do. When you keep Him first, as Jesus declared, "But seek *first* His kingdom and His righteousness…*all these things will be added to you*" (Matthew 6:33 NASB). By keeping first things first, you bring your life into the order God has established. God adds the "things" to you when the foundation is in place to be built upon.

Revelation causes motivation. We live by faith, and walking out and operating out of that faith is our responsibility. We are the ones who have to create and establish an atmosphere that is focused on God and based on the principles of His Word. The principle of first fruits is part of that active walking out our faith in operation to release the promises of God. The *first* sets the precedent for the rest.

CHAPTER 6

GOD'S PATTERNS:
ONE FOR MANY

From the first chapter of Genesis throughout the entire Old Testament, we see patterns. Many times I've heard it said that the Old Testament is the New concealed, and the New Testament is the Old revealed. Have you ever heard that? It is referring to the fact that most of what we see in the Old Testament is a "type and shadow" of what is revealed in the New Testament, our New Covenant in Christ Jesus.

In the book of Hebrews, speaking of the priests of the Old Covenant, the writer says,

> They serve at a sanctuary that is a copy and shadow of what is in heaven. This is why Moses was warned when he was about to build the tabernacle: "See to it that you make everything according to the pattern shown you on the mountain." But the ministry Jesus has received is as superior to theirs as the covenant of which he is mediator is superior to the old one, and it is founded on better promises (Hebrews 8:5-6 NIV).

The New Covenant is founded on better promises because it is the fulfillment of what was patterned before. The Old Testament was a pattern. God sets everything in place, line upon line, and precept upon precept.

This is shown very clearly in Exodus 25. God is giving Moses the exact instructions—to the smallest detail—of how things are to be made, from the ephods and breastplates the priests would wear, to the Ark of the Covenant, to the table and lamp stand, and the Tabernacle itself. "Then have them make a sanctuary for me, and I will dwell among them. Make this tabernacle and all its furnishings exactly like the pattern I will show you" (v. 8-9 NIV).

Paul said, "Nevertheless, death reigned from the time of Adam to the time of Moses, even over those who did not sin by breaking a command, as did Adam, who was a pattern of the one to come" (Romans 5:14 NIV). Adam was a pattern of Christ, the One to come. It is from His correlation to Adam that Christ called Himself not only the Son of God, but frequently, the Son of Man.

Just as the High Priests of old would enter through the veil on the Day of Atonement to place blood on the altar within the Holy of Holies, God set up the Tabernacle and the Day of Atonement as a pattern for the One High Priest who would enter beyond the veil and make atonement for us all.

Jesus left His throne, left the precious presence of His Father and the Holy Spirit, and was born of a woman in a common barn. He was crucified and buried in a borrowed tomb, and He arose again on the third day. Soon after, He saw Mary in the garden. When she recognized Her Messiah, she longed to touch Him as she had many times before. But He told her, "Do not hold on to me, for I have not yet returned to the Father. Go instead to my brothers and tell them, 'I am returning to

my Father and your Father, to my God and your God'"
(John 20:17 NIV).

Why did He have to ascend to Heaven first? To fulfill
the pattern of what was before. Sin did not originate on
earth; rebellion began first in Heaven. Jesus completed
the work of the High Priest, making atonement for us
all, by placing His own precious blood upon the altar
of Heaven.

THE ROOT OF IT ALL

First fruits is also part of God's pattern. Remember
that first fruits means the first in place, order and rank; the
beginning, chief or principle thing. We have to keep
things in their proper order. The problem is, we try to get
the results without following the pattern. If I were to sit
down and try to make my own clothes for example, I
would need a pattern to even know where to begin. And
if I didn't have a pattern to work from, there is no way I'd
end up with anything I'd wear in public! Similarly, if a
contractor were to build a house without a blue print, a
plan, or a pattern, that house would probably fall down.

Notice what Romans 8:29 says of Jesus, "For whom
he did fore-know, he also did predestinate to be
conformed to the image of his Son, that he might be the
firstborn among many brethren." So Jesus was a "first."
He was the firstborn among many brethren—those who
would come to call upon His name and be called children
of God. As 1 Corinthians 15:23 says, "But every man in
his own order; Christ the firstfruits; afterward they that

are Christ's at His coming."

Paul called Jesus the firstborn of many brethren, and in Corinthians he called Him the first fruits. Following the "pattern" set out in Exodus 22:29 (NIV), "You must give me the firstborn of your sons," Jesus, therefore, is the "part," that redeems the whole, the root that governs the rest. "If the part of the dough offered as firstfruits is holy, then the whole batch is holy; if the root is holy, so are the branches" (Romans 11:16 NIV). Jesus fulfilled God's pattern of one for many, the first fruits redeeming and blessing those who were yet to come.

Why does our day, our week, our year get out of order? Because we're out of God's order of first fruits. When we take the first fruits for our own use, we are out of order, therefore everything else is likewise out of order. The root governs the rest. This principle can even apply to your relationships. It was Jewish custom and tradition for the new bride and groom to take the first *year* off for their honeymoon. They clearly understood God's pattern that the root governs the rest.

People ask me why my husband and I set January aside as a season of private and corporate fasting, giving, and prayer. God set the Feast of First Fruits as the beginning of things for Israel. Though I recognize that God has a different "calendar" and understand the history of it, for most of us the calendar we live by starts with the month of January. We are offering up that first month unto the Lord to establish what happens in the rest of the year.

By presenting God the firstfruits: the first part of your day, the first month of the year, the first of your increase, you are saying "I present this as holy, consecrated to the Lord…and I cannot touch it." It governs everything else that operates in your life.

When this begins to hit your spirit, you'll understand that God is not trying to take something *from* you. He has made a pattern for us to follow in order to walk in the abundant life He promised through Christ Jesus. As we begin to get revelation of this pattern in our hearts, we will be positioned to receive! First fruits not only represents a promise that is to come in your life, it is the key that unlocks many other doors.

DO NOT TOUCH!

Paul instructed the Philippians saying, "Join with others in following my example, brothers, and take note of those who live according to the pattern we gave you" (Philippians 3:17 NIV). I find it interesting that he continued that instruction saying, "For, as I have often told you before and now say again even with tears, many live as enemies of the cross of Christ. Their destiny is destruction…their mind is on earthly things" (v. 19).

Remember, carnal mindedness brings death to things in your life. But following the patterns and principles of God, and keeping first things first by seeking first His kingdom, brings life.

The Hebrew word for devoted things and accursed things is the same, *cherem,* or the root *charam.* Both

86

mean the irrevocable giving over to the Lord, something that is to be utterly destroyed. Let's look again at Leviticus 27:28-29:

> Notwithstanding no devoted thing, that a man shall devote unto the LORD of all that he hath, both of man and beast, and of the field of his possession, shall be sold or redeemed: every devoted thing is *most holy* unto the LORD. None devoted, which shall be devoted of men, shall be redeemed; but shall surely be put to death.

SAUL UNWILLING

In 1 Samuel 15, God sent word to king Saul through the prophet Samuel that He intended to "punish the Amalekites for what they did to Israel when they waylaid them as they came up from Egypt" (v. 2 NIV). Then the Lord instructed Saul saying, "Now go, attack the Amalekites and totally destroy everything that belongs to them. Do not spare them; put to death men and women, children and infants, cattle and sheep, camels and donkeys" (v. 3).

Saul was obedient to the Lord and attacked the Amalekites, and God gave him victory "from Havilah to Shur, to the east of Egypt" (v. 7). However, though God told Saul to completely wipe out every Amalekite, even their cattle, sheep and other livestock, Saul chose to keep the king of the Amalekites alive as well as "the best of the sheep and cattle, the fat calves and lambs—everything that was good. These they were unwilling to destroy completely" (v. 9).

Saul's unwillingness to obey deeply grieved the Lord. When Samuel confronted Saul with the word of the Lord about his disobedience, Samuel asked, "Why did you not obey the Lord? Why did you pounce on the plunder and do evil in the eyes of the Lord?"

Saul replied, "The soldiers took sheep and cattle from the plunder, the best of what was devoted to God, in order to sacrifice them to the LORD your God at Gilgal" (v. 21).

Saul knew that all of the plunder was *devoted* to the Lord—devoted to destruction. Yet, he and his men spared the best of what God said to destroy—for their own use. You are probably familiar with the next verse, "But Samuel replied: 'Does the LORD delight in burnt offerings and sacrifices as much as in obeying the voice of the LORD? To obey is better than sacrifice, and to heed is better than the fat of rams'" (v. 22 NIV).

This example, though not specifically about a first fruits offering, does illustrate how very serious God is about things He calls devoted. The Amalekites were devoted to destruction, and for Israel to take anything that was so devoted and use it for their own use—even to make sacrifices unto the Lord—was completely unacceptable to God. Saul lost his kingdom and was tormented the rest of his days, and due to his disobedience, the

Amalekites continued to be an issue for Israel.

As we read previously in Exodus 34:20, "Redeem the firstborn donkey with a lamb, but if you do not redeem it, break its neck" (NIV). It is better to destroy something that is devoted to the Lord rather than keep it for your own use. Holy things belong to the Lord, and the Lord calls first fruits or first things holy.

JOSHUA AT AI

As I have said before, it is not so much what we're doing wrong, as it is that we're not doing enough of what is right. When things aren't going well, it is easy to get into a religious mindset, thinking that if you only pray more…fast more…do this or do that more…but the problem is often that things are out of order in your life. If the pattern is wrong you can never be positioned for the promise. If the pattern is wrong, it could be bringing death to things in your life that should be abundant.

For forty years the children of Israel had wandered, watching the older generation gradually pass away, until the generation of promise was all that was left. Camped across the Jordan from Jericho, Moses made his way to a high mountain to seek the Lord once more. From there, the Lord showed him the land of promise:

> …from Gilead to Dan, all of Naphtali,
> the territory of Ephraim and Manasseh,
> all the land of Judah as far as the western
> sea, the Negev and the whole region

from the Valley of Jericho, the City of Palms, as far as Zoar. Then the LORD said to him, "This is the land I promised on oath to Abraham, Isaac and Jacob when I said, 'I will give it to your descendants. I have let you see it with your eyes, but you will not cross over into it" (Deuteronomy 34:1-4 NIV).

The generation that was to walk into that promise would do so under Joshua's leadership, not Moses'. They marched forth, following God's instructions, and the walls of the most powerful city around crumbled to the ground before them. Just before the shout went up, Joshua warned the people saying,

"But keep away from the devoted things, so that you will not bring about your own destruction by taking any of them. Otherwise you will make the camp of Israel liable to destruction and bring trouble on it. All the silver and gold and the articles of bronze and iron are sacred to the LORD and must go into his treasury" (Joshua 6:18-19 NIV).

With the exception of Rahab and her family, who were protected because she had helped Joshua's spies, the army of Israel "devoted the city to the Lord and destroyed with the sword every living thing in it" (v. 21 NIV).

It was a great victory for the Lord, and for the people of Israel; or so it seemed. The very next city they were to conquer was Ai. The spies told Joshua they only needed about 3000 of the fighting men to take the city. But to Israel's dismay, "they were routed by the men of Ai, who killed about thirty-six of them. They chased the Israelites from the city gate as far as the stone quarries and struck them down on the slopes. At this the hearts of the people melted and became like water" (Joshua 7:4-5 NIV).

How could the greatest city fall before them, and the weakest one send them running? After Jericho, the Lord was with Joshua and "his fame spread throughout the land." What changed?

The answer is found in the first verse of Joshua chapter 7, "But the Israelites acted unfaithfully in regard to the devoted things [the accursed things]; Achan son of Carmi, the son of Zimri, the son of Zerah, of the tribe of Judah, took some of them. So the LORD's anger burned against Israel" (NIV). Instead of marching out in God's favor, they had gone up against their enemy without His protection. Achan was in possession of an accursed thing—of holy things—and God's blessing could not rest on Israel.

Though Joshua cried out to God in prayer, God answered him and said,

Stand up! What are you doing down on

your face? Israel has sinned; they have violated my covenant, which I commanded them to keep. They have taken some of the devoted things; they have stolen, they have lied, they have put them with their own possessions. That is why the Israelites cannot stand against their enemies; they turn their backs and run because they have been made liable to destruction. I will not be with you anymore unless you destroy whatever among you is devoted to destruction (Joshua 7:10-12 NIV).

I never want to experience the Lord's absence. I cannot imagine trying to do anything without the Lord being with me. Look at the destruction wrought by just one man's disobedience. One man touched the holy things. One man took some of the devoted things and put them with his own belongings, yet God said, "Israel has sinned." There was sin in the camp, and the entire camp was subject to the results of that accursed thing. When it was discovered that Achan was the one who had taken the devoted things, he and his entire family, children and all, were killed. When God calls something a holy thing, it belongs to Him. There is death where there should be abundant life anytime things are out of order.

Do you know why a lot of us cannot stand before our enemies? Perhaps it is because we have touched

things that belong to God and when we do, we can remove the hedge of protection from our lives. The Israelites walked into Jericho with abundant favor. God was with them. "For thou, Lord, wilt bless the righteous; with favor wilt thou compass him as with a shield" (Psalm 5:12). But when one man took the holy things for himself, he brought a curse on his family, as well as on Israel.

When we obey, we are blessed; when we do not, we open ourselves to demonic activity—not unlike Saul, whose willful disobedience lost him the kingdom and brought him a tormenting spirit. That does not mean God is cursing you; it means that by touching something holy, you literally open the door to demonic spirits in your life. As with Saul, sacrifice is not what pleases God–obedience does. Your obedience gets you in line with the pattern, which positions you for the promise. As Proverbs 10:22 declares, "The blessing of the Lord, it maketh rich, and he addeth no sorrow with it."

CHAPTER 7

MYSTERY OF CAIN'S OFFERING

In twenty-three years of studying God's Word every day, I still have only scratched the surface. But when something really puzzles me, I find that I just can't let it go until I dig deeper and get a better understanding of it.

The difference between Cain's offering and Abel's offering had been such a mystery to me for a long time. I could not figure out what it was about Cain's offering that was unacceptable to the Lord. And why did Cain become so angry? As I began to gain more insight into the principle of first fruits, it all started making more sense.

It is possible that Cain and Abel were twins. We definitely know they were brothers, born to Adam and Eve. I think it is interesting to notice what Eve said after Cain was delivered: "I have gotten a manchild with the help of the LORD" (Genesis 4:1 NASB). Eve had been promised a son, one whose heel would crush the serpent's head. If you think about it, I'm sure she was still disgusted with that serpent! It is possible she thought Cain was the fulfillment of that promise, but it seems she really only gave partial thanks to God for the birth of her first-born son. That makes me wonder if Cain didn't already have issues from the day he took his first breath.

When the boys grew older, Cain began to work the ground, plowing, planting, and collecting a harvest from the various crops and trees. Abel began breeding and raising a herd of sheep, since man was apparently no longer on the vegetable-only Genesis diet that was enjoyed in the Garden of Eden before the Fall.

Commentators generally agree that God must have given some form of worship and oblation instructions to that very first family. Though no specifics are given in that regard, I believe God had established a pattern with Adam and Eve, explaining the nature of offerings to be made unto the Lord, and that pattern has continued throughout the generations. It is also clear that Adam, Eve, and even their children were able to hear the voice of the Lord and worship Him. Notice what happens after the first recorded offering:

> And in process of time it came to pass, that Cain brought of the fruit of the ground an offering unto the LORD. And Abel, he also brought of the firstlings of his flock and of the fat thereof. And the LORD had respect unto Abel and to his offering: But unto Cain and to his offering he had not respect. And Cain was very wroth, and his countenance fell (Genesis 4:3-5).

ABEL'S OFFERING

It would seem that the phrase, "in process of time," relates to the end or beginning of something. Whether it was the beginning of a week, month or year is unclear. It is also not stated exactly what type of offering was required, but we can see that Abel brought a first fruits offering. He brought of the "firstlings of his flock." Giving a first fruits offering requires faith, and Abel demonstrated this faith, which was apparently pleasing to the Lord. As the writer of Hebrews recorded, "By faith Abel offered God a better sacrifice than Cain did. By faith he was commended as a righteous man, when God spoke well of his offerings" (Hebrews 11:4 NIV).

Hebrews goes on to say that, "Without faith it is impossible to please God, because anyone who comes to him must believe that he exists and that he rewards those who earnestly seek him" (Hebrews 11:6). The first fruits offering is based on faith: faith in the fact that the root governs the rest...faith that giving God the whole of the first sets the course for blessings to be released on the rest...faith that God is a rewarder of those who earnestly seek Him.

It was said of Abraham that he *believed God*. That faith was credited to him as righteousness, or right standing with God (see Genesis 15:6). Paul expounds on this further in Romans 4:18-22. In the Amplified version it says:

> [For Abraham, human reason for] hope being gone, hoped in faith that he should become the father of many nations, as he had been promised, "So [numberless] shall your descendants be." He did not weaken in faith when he considered the [utter] impotence of his own

body, which was as good as dead because
he was about a hundred years old, or
[when he considered] the barrenness of
Sarah's [deadened] womb.

No unbelief or distrust made him
waver (doubtingly question) concerning
the promise of God, but he grew strong
and was empowered by faith as he gave
praise and glory to God, fully satisfied
and assured that God was able and
mighty to keep His word and to do what
He had promised.

That is why his faith was credited to
him as righteousness (right standing with
God).

So, going by what was said of Abraham, it is clear
that the faith Abel demonstrated in preparing a first fruits
offering is what pleased the Lord, and was also credited
to him as righteousness, as we see in Hebrews 11:4. What
does *righteous* mean? It doesn't mean that he was simply
a good man, or that he was handsome, or charismatic in
his personality. It means Abel was in right standing with
God. It means Abel placed God first, in the right place.
Abel followed the pattern. He brought a first fruits
offering—and because of his faith in that act of worship
and acknowledging that it was not by his own hand that
he was prosperous in raising sheep, but by God's hand
that he was blessed, he was counted as a righteous man.

CAIN'S OFFERING

Once again I say it is not that we are doing something wrong, but that we are not doing *enough* of what is right. Did Cain bring an offering? Yes, he brought "of the fruit of the ground an offering" to give the Lord. But it was a *partial* offering.

First of all, without the shedding of blood there is no forgiveness of sins (see Hebrews 9:22). Abel's offering involved bloodshed, but Cain's offering was from the cursed ground (see Genesis 3:17). A first fruits offering is not a sin offering, but coming before God as he did, it was as if Cain was presenting his offering based on his own worthiness, rather than by God's mercy. He presented the work of his own toil, of his own hands, no doubt bringing choice fruits for his offering. Some believe he may have brought fine flour, frankincense and olive oil common for a general gratitude offering, or even a tithe—but not *first* fruits; "And whatsoever is first ripe in the land, which they shall bring unto the Lord..." (Numbers 18:13). Because he gave only a part and not in faith, God was not pleased.

I can imagine Cain coming with his offering, one that he probably took great pride in preparing and working to arrange. As it was in the Old Testament, when God accepted an offering that was laid upon the altar, He consumed it with fire from heaven. Imagine the feeling of seeing your brother's messy, bloody pile of fat portions from slaughtered lambs lying there next to the bodies of the lambs themselves! Then imagine God consuming that messy offering with fire while your beautiful arrangement lay untouched. The burning fat and meat was a sweet aroma to God, but it was the smell of death to Cain as his offering was unaccepted.

The Bible says Cain's countenance fell. His face began to reveal what was in his heart—disgust, disappointment and anger that his labor had been for nothing. This must have intensified in the days, and weeks, and possibly months to come, as he began to observe the blessings of God manifesting in his brother Abel's life, while Cain continued to toil with the soil.

THE RIGHT PATTERN

Cain worshiped God according to what he *thought* was enough. His worship had a "form of godliness" but denied "the power thereof" (see 2 Timothy 3:5). In other words, it "looked good" but he failed to tap into the power of the blessing through the power of complete and total faith in God.

How many of us think we can come and worship God in our own way? How many of us think, "We are doing enough. We show up every Sunday and put our tithe in the offering plate?" Are we supposed to worship God according to the dictates of our own thoughts and imaginations, or according to the patterns and principles that He has established?

It is interesting that the first offering of this kind is found in Genesis. Think about what happened in the Garden of Eden. "And the LORD God made all kinds of trees grow out of the ground—trees that were pleasing to the eye and good for food. In the middle of the garden were the tree of life and the tree of the knowledge of good and evil" (Genesis 2:9 NIV). God told Adam that he could eat from any other tree in the garden, but "you must not eat from the tree of the knowledge of good and evil, for when you eat of it you will surely die" (v. 17).

Eve told the serpent that God said not to "touch it" or they would "surely die." She knew what God said, but after the enemy twisted the Word of God a little, notice what happens: "When the woman saw that the fruit of the tree was good for food and pleasing to the eye, and also desirable for gaining wisdom, she took some and ate it" (Genesis 3:6 NIV). How many times do we look at our "firsts" and decide it is good for us—it is good for food or to buy what we want...it is nice to look at for our own use...and so on? Yet doing so will "surely" bring death rather than abundance to our lives.

As time passed, Cain became very jealous of the prosperity and of the blessing of the Lord on Abel's life. Seeing Cain's condition, God spoke directly to him, giving him another chance; "Then the LORD said to Cain, 'Why are you angry? Why is your face downcast? If you do what is right, will you not be accepted? But if you do not do what is right, sin is crouching at your door; it desires to have you, but you must master it'" (Genesis 4:6-7 NIV).

God gave Cain the opportunity to *follow the pattern of what was right*; the pattern demonstrated by his brother Abel whose first fruits offering was given in faith. If Cain did what was *right* his offering would be accepted. Sadly, instead of humbling himself and being taught of the Lord, he developed an unteachable spirit, and in turning from God he opened the door to sin. Like Saul, Cain chose to disobey God, thereby opening the door to demonic spirits, and it drove him to kill his innocent brother.

Jude refers to this tragedy later on, in warning against those who are apostate, saying, "Woe to them! They have taken the way of Cain; they have rushed for profit into Balaam's error; they have been destroyed in Korah's rebellion" (Jude 1:11 NIV). John also warns us to "not be like Cain who [took his nature and got his motivation] from the evil one and slew his brother. And why did he slay him? Because his deeds (activities, works) were wicked and malicious and his brother's were righteous (virtuous)" (1 John 3:12 AMP).

BEWARE OF THE "CAIN SPIRIT"

We are all capable of operating in the "Cain spirit." It is a matter of either walking in the flesh and fulfilling the desires thereof, or putting God first in everything and walking according to the Spirit of God, and fulfilling His desires.

What we call the "Early church" began on the day of Pentecost, when the Holy Spirit was poured out in such a mighty way, as Joel had prophesied. When other Jews who were gathered in the city saw these people baptized in the Spirit, they thought they were drunk. This prompted Peter's powerful address to the crowd, drawing all to repentance. Acts 2:41 notes, "Those who accepted his message were baptized, and about three thousand were added to their number that day" (NIV).

It is in the following verses that we see why those who were part of the Early church had such tremendous power:

> They devoted themselves to the apostles' teaching and to the fellowship, to the breaking of bread and to prayer. Everyone was filled with awe, and many wonders and miraculous signs were done by the apostles. All the believers were together and had everything in common. Selling their possessions and goods, they gave to anyone as he had need. Every day they continued to meet together in the temple courts. They broke bread in their homes and ate together with glad and sincere hearts, praising God and enjoying the favor of all the people. And the Lord added to their number daily those who were being saved (Acts 2:42-47 NIV).

They operated according to the Spirit, not the flesh, and there was life in abundance! Jesus healed the sick, cast out demons and raised the dead, and told us that we—His disciples—would do even greater things. In the Early church, even Peter's shadow falling on a sick person resulted in healing!

They gave freely to those who had need, and had sold their possessions so that they had all things common.

> All the believers were one in heart and mind. No one claimed that any of his possessions was his own, but they shared everything they had. With great power the apostles continued to testify to the resurrection of the Lord Jesus, and much grace was upon them all. There were no needy persons among them. For from time to time those who owned lands or houses sold them, brought the money from the sales and put it at the apostles' feet, and it was distributed to anyone as he had need. (Acts 4:32-35 NIV).

They shared all things equally for the good of the whole and for the establishment of God's Kingdom. That was their utmost priority. That was their "first fruits" and their blessings were abundant.

Then entered the Cain spirit; that spirit which says, "I can do it my way...I can worship God in a way that makes sense to me and still be blessed." I believe Luke, the writer of the book of Acts, must have been rather amazed by what he saw next. As he wrote to Theophilus in Acts chapter 5: "Now a man named Ananias, together with his wife Sapphira, also sold a piece of property. With his wife's full knowledge he kept back part of the money for himself, but brought the rest and put it at the apostles' feet" (v. 1, 2).

That seems fair enough, right? The man wanted to look after his own needs for the future. Since the whole group was being so blessed, he probably got way more for his property than he expected to receive. So...who would know the difference? Certainly not that ex-fisherman-turned-apostle Peter, right? What does he know?

As Ananias laid his partial gift at Peter's feet, Peter said,

> "Ananias, how is it that Satan has so filled your heart that you have lied to the Holy Spirit and have kept for yourself some of the money you received for the land? Didn't it belong to you before it was sold? And after it was sold, wasn't the money at your disposal? What made you think of doing such a thing? You have not lied to men but to God." When Ananias heard this, he fell down and died (Acts 5:3-5 NIV).

Ananias didn't bank on the Holy Spirit *speaking* to Peter. Moments later, when Sapphira walked in, she too dropped dead at hearing Peter's words and her body was carried out.

The Early church had power because they did things by the pattern. They had unity and they had things in their right order, first things first. They kept the Main Thing—the main thing! Was there provision? Yes. Did they ever lack anything? Never. Jesus at one point sent His disciples out with nothing, yet they had everything they needed by relying on Him. They understood God's power and they understood the pattern.

It seems cruel that those two were killed in such a manner after giving—I mean, they *did* give. But like Cain, they gave what they thought would be right— what's worse, they lied about the rest. Everyone else was giving of the *whole*, but they *withheld* and said it was the whole. Remember, one of the reasons for lack that I explained earlier was withholding, and Ananias and his wife quickly lacked life!

They touched what was holy. They indicated that they were giving a first thing, a first fruit, which the Lord claims as His own. But they did not. When you live spiritually minded—following God's pattern, there is life. On the contrary, when you live carnally minded, touching things that are holy, there is death.

NO CONDEMNATION

"There is therefore now no condemnation to them which are in Christ Jesus, who walk not after the flesh, but after the Spirit" (Romans 8:1). I am not sharing these examples to bring condemnation, but to bring clarity. God is serious about first things. Life abundant or lack abundant—the choice is ours to make. I want you to become positioned to receive the blessings of God, learning to distinguish the difference between merely giving an offering of what "seems good at the time," and the power that giving the first fruits offering will release in your life. God knows what's best for us. He wants to bless you—to give you the power and anointing to get wealth—to establish His covenant. We are set free through the blood of Jesus, but the principle that the root establishes the rest is still in effect. This is why first fruits is so vital and key for you to understand and activate in your life. The root establishes or governs the rest. First fruits is the whole of the first, and God sees that as "holy." What you do with all "firsts" governs what occurs with the rest.

I am thankful God gives second chances! Like Cain, God gives us the space and prompting to examine our hearts "and do well." God's promises are not given on the basis of any "good works" we do. The first fruits offering is not about positioning ourselves to "win" God's acceptance and favor. It is about positioning ourselves to "release" God's blessings—acting in faith in order to see them manifest in our lives. It is your faith in Him that brings God's promises to you.

CHAPTER 8

BLESSINGS AT REST

According to what John wrote in the Book of Revelation, our testimonies are powerful tools against the enemy (see Revelation 12:11). I used to be amazed at the awesome things God did in my life, and in the lives of others who joined Randy and me in giving the offering of first fruits. While I still rejoice in the mighty things God does—I have to admit I have come to *expect* magnificent blessings to be released in the lives of people who follow this principle. That is not intended to sound arrogant at all; but time and experience of seeing God's faithfulness creates that expectation. As we read in the first chapter, when you are obedient, when you follow God's patterns, you will be blessed. You will walk in the life *more abundantly* that Jesus spoke of.

That's why, in the next few chapters, I want to share with you some powerful testimonies of how people from all different situations and walks of life have overcome lack and defeat by exercising their faith in God by giving first fruits offerings. Their testimonies demonstrate what God has done in the lives of those who have heard the teaching, embraced it, and been incredibly blessed as a result. I believe their stories will begin to stir your spirit and increase your faith.

For example, we received a hand-written note from a man who had been separated from his wife for nearly two years. He writes, "Last January I gave my first fruits offering for the very first time. The devil fought me every step of the way in making my decision, but I decided to listen to the voice of God instead and I offered my first week's pay."

Notice the incredible blessings that were released in his life over the course of that same year. He continues, "I saw my income increase $20,000 after I received a promotion, my wife and I have reconciled after being apart for two years, my wife's health has been restored, we have purchased a new home, and God has been blessing other members of our family as well."

I love how moved this man was by the overflowing abundance of the blessings of God in his life. He concludes his letter, "God has been so good that, even as I write this letter, tears of joy are coming down my face. To God be the glory."

The enemy had stolen from this man's life on many sides, but after his first fruits offering, his entire situation turned around. Instead of leaving the door open for the enemy, he received promotion…reconciliation…healing…land and more!

THE PRIEST WILL TAKE THE BASKET

I have explained the pattern of first fruits, but how did God intend for the first fruits to be presented? As you may have already guessed, there is a pattern for that as well. God originally established that the first fruits offering was to be brought to the priests. In the book of the "second law," or Deuteronomy as we know it, Moses spent much time giving clear detail as he repeated the laws God had given Israel. In chapter 26 he begins,

When you have entered the land the LORD your God is giving you as an inheritance and have taken possession of it and settled in it, take some of the firstfruits of all that you produce from the soil of the land the LORD your God is giving you and put them in a basket. Then go to the place the LORD your God will choose as a dwelling for his Name and say to the priest in office at the time, "I declare today to the LORD your God that I have come to the land the LORD swore to our forefathers to give us."

The priest shall take the basket from your hands and set it down in front of the altar of the LORD your God (Deuteronomy 26:1-4 NIV).

Once they handed the priest the first fruits offering they were to proclaim the story of Isaac's journey into Egypt, how his descendants became a great nation, and the resulting slavery and their suffering. Then they verbally acknowledged how…

"…The LORD brought us out of Egypt with a mighty hand and an outstretched arm, with great terror and with miraculous signs and wonders. He brought us

112

to this place and gave us this land, a land
flowing with milk and honey; and now I
bring the firstfruits of the soil that you, O
LORD, have given me." (Deuteronomy
26:8-10)

Finally, they were instructed to: "Place the basket
before the LORD your God and bow down before
him. And you and the Levites and the aliens among you
shall rejoice in all the good things the LORD your
God has given to you and your household" (Deuteronomy 26:10-11).

Other offerings of the first sheaves of wheat were for
the land, but the first fruits offering described here
related to the Feast. I can imagine the people marking
their crops, waiting for those first fruits to mature and
ripen—and how they must have naturally desired a taste
of that year's very first grapes, figs, wheat, barley,
pomegranates, olives, and dates. But they would put God
first, taking their baskets out, separating each different
fruit within the basket with some leaves, and presenting
the best of the best unto the Lord.

But—what happened to all those baskets of fruit
afterwards? They were not consumed by fire. God didn't
come down and eat them. So who did? The priests did.
As God told Aaron, "All the land's firstfruits that they
bring to the LORD will be yours. Everyone in your
household who is ceremonially clean may eat it"
(Numbers 18:13 NIV). Like other offerings, the first

fruits offerings were part of what was used to support and feed those who ministered God's Word to the people. I'm going to give you a lot of scripture in this chapter because I want you to see this pattern. When explaining the appointed feasts to Moses, God said:

> Speak to the Israelites and say to them: "When you enter the land I am going to give you and you reap its harvest, bring to the priest a sheaf of the first grain you harvest. He is to wave the sheaf before the LORD so it will be accepted on your behalf; the priest is to wave it on the day after the Sabbath. ... This is to be a lasting ordinance for the generations to come, wherever you live.
>
> From the day after the Sabbath, the day you brought the sheaf of the wave offering, count off seven full weeks. Count off fifty days up to the day after the seventh Sabbath, and then present an offering of new grain to the LORD. From wherever you live, bring two loaves made of two-tenths of an ephah of fine flour, baked with yeast, as a wave offering of firstfruits to the LORD...Then sacrifice one male goat for a sin offering and two lambs, each a year old, for a fellowship offering. The

priest is to wave the two lambs before the LORD as a wave offering, together with the bread of the firstfruits. They are a sacred offering to the LORD for the priest…This is to be a lasting ordinance for the generations to come, wherever you live (Leviticus 23:10-21 NIV).

Bringing the first fruits offering to the priests was a lasting ordinance for the generations. Notice what God says of the Levites:

After you have purified the Levites and presented them as a wave offering, they are to come to do their work at the Tent of Meeting. They are the Israelites who are to be given wholly to me. I have taken them as my own in place of the firstborn, the first male offspring from every Israelite woman. Every firstborn male in Israel, whether man or animal, is mine. When I struck down all the firstborn in Egypt, I set them apart for myself. And I have taken the Levites in place of all the firstborn sons in Israel. Of all the Israelites, I have given the Levites as gifts to Aaron and his sons to do the work at the Tent of Meeting on behalf of the Israelites and to make atonement for them so that no plague will strike the Israelites when they go near the sanctuary (Numbers 8:15-19 NIV).

The Levites serving in such manner actually helped prevent plagues from striking the Israelites. As I stated before, God is not trying to hold anything back from you...He is trying to get things *to* you. Anything that is a first, a first thing, a first fruit, a first born, a devoted thing, God always lays claim to it. It belongs to God—not a portion of it—but the whole thing. God sees the first thing as the root that governs all the rest.

WHY THE PRIESTS?

God's Word is full of patterns, and the manner in which the first fruits were to be presented to the Lord was no different. In the Old Testament, the offerings were given to the priests and Levites so that they could be devoted to the work of the Lord and carry out His instructions for the people. But what was significant in the Old Testament about bringing the first fruits offering to the priests in such a manner? How did that benefit the one who brought the offering?

The key is found in the words of God to Ezekiel, "And the first of all the firstfruits of all things, and every oblation of all, of every sort of your oblations, shall be the priest's: ye shall also give unto the priest the first of your dough, *that he may cause the blessing to rest in thine house*" (Ezekiel 44:30; emphasis added).

Under the Old Covenant, the priest received the first fruits offering and waved it before the Lord as a means of presenting it to God. He then prayed to release the blessings of the Lord over the house of the one who presented the offering.

But let's take this apart a little. It says that the priest would cause the blessing to rest on your *house*. The first tendency is to think of the physical building in which you dwell. But the Israelites were living in tents at the time. The Hebrew term for house or household in this verse is *bayith*, meaning family. It comes from the root word *banah*, which means to build. The blessing would rest not on your dwelling, but on your family…on your lineage…your children, grandchildren, their kids and grandkids and so on.

Joshua put a choice before the Israelites to choose who they would serve, the Lord or other gods. Then he gave his choice: "As for me and my house, we will serve the Lord" (Joshua 24:15). Again, we tend to think "and my house" may include the husband, wife, and kids living there at the time. But actually it means generation after generation.

Not all denominations have a "priesthood" any longer, nor do the priests and leaders live off the fruits and slaughtered animals of the sacrifice. The equivalent today would be bringing your first fruits offering to the man or woman of God with whom you are in covenant. I've had people ask me about how they can give first fruits at their church if their leader doesn't know or understand the principle. Remember, the man or woman of God is blessed by your giving first fruits. One dear woman wrote to us recently that she had never heard of first fruits before hearing me teach the principle on our program. She says,

> I was really excited and went online and printed the teaching. That evening I shared it with my husband. He had just received his two-week paycheck and said, "I believe we need to do this." He gave that entire check as a first fruits offering. The next week he received a check from someone who said she didn't know why she sent it...she just knew that she should! The next week I took my 1-week paycheck and my tithe and gave it to my pastor—with the explanation that it was a first fruits offering. He was overwhelmed. I said, "This is something God has told us to do." The ripples of the pond are going out!

This woman had the opportunity to share a life-giving principle with the man of God appointed to her congregation, and he was able to pronounce a blessing over her household. But notice that this is not a one-time blessing. It doesn't mean that you're blessed for a day or two after you give your first fruits. The testimonies in my own life, and those I read on a regular basis that come from other people tell of blessings that continue far beyond the time of the offering. That is because the priest (or man/woman of God) causes the blessing to *rest* on your household.

The Hebrew word for blessing in this text is *berakah*, meaning by implication, prosperity. It comes from the root word *barak*, meaning to kneel, to bless God as an act of adoration, and also, to bless man. Remember, prosperity does not just mean financial increase. Prosperity is a wholeness word that means every part of your life. Notice that the *blessing*, the *berakah* was not promised to come and go, but to rest or (in Hebrew) it was to *nuwach*, meaning to stay, settle down or to fall in place.

When you get things in the right order, by the right pattern, the blessing doesn't just come by you, but the blessing settles down and it stays in place. It means the enemy might come after you, but he's not going to destroy you. I am living proof of that fact. I believe the reason the ministry God has called me to has prospered as it has, is a result of living my life according to the pattern He has revealed; laying the foundation of first fruits and growing from there.

I have tried to build everything in my life on the foundation of God's order and God's pattern with the knowledge I had at the time. There are many blessings in my life—many of which I will share with you in these pages. I am not ashamed of those blessings because they are a result of following the patterns of God; keeping the

Main Thing the main thing. I'm not just talking about financial prosperity either—but blessings that affect every bit of my life and those of my family and generations to come. I am also encouraged *daily* when I see faithful men and women of God bringing their first fruits offerings to Randy and me as the leaders of Without Walls—and we proclaim the blessings of God over their lives.

Under the New Covenant, Jesus is our High Priest; "Moses was faithful as a servant in all God's house, testifying to what would be said in the future. But Christ is faithful as a son over God's house. And we are his house, if we hold on to our courage and the hope of which we boast" (Hebrews 3:5-6 NIV). Paul told the disciples to "keep watch over yourselves and all the flock of which the Holy Spirit has made you overseers. Be shepherds of the church of God, which he bought with his own blood" (Acts 20:28 NIV).

WHERE YOUR TREASURE IS

Another benefit of the first fruits offering comes from what it does for the one receiving it. The Bibles says that, "Moreover he commanded the people that dwelt in Jerusalem to give the portion of the priests and the Levites, that they might be encouraged in the law of the LORD" (2 Chronicles 31:4). Other versions say, "to give the portion due to the priests and the Levites, that they might devote themselves to the law of the LORD" (NASB).

The writer of Hebrews said, "Obey your leaders and

120

submit to their authority. They keep watch over you as men who must give an account. Obey them so that their work will be a joy, not a burden, for that would be of no advantage to you." (Hebrews 13:17 NIV). The men and women of God whom He has called to preach His Word and watch over His flock are positioned to watch over your soul. Locked up in them is a vision. It is imperative that people who are called to a ministry also help protect and bless that ministry, not unlike Aaron and Hur supporting Moses in the battle. Their vision is locked up in the womb of that man or woman of God. We know what Proverbs 29:18 declares, "Where there is no vision, the people perish."

Jesus warned, "Do not store up for yourselves treasures on earth, where moth and rust destroy, and where thieves break in and steal. But store up for yourselves treasures in heaven, where moth and rust do not destroy, and where thieves do not break in and steal. For where your treasure is, there your heart will be also" (Matthew 6:19-21 NIV).

You cannot be connected without treasure. God uses your gifts, your treasure, to connect you in covenant with the ministry. You are drawn to or in covenant with ministries because your heart identifies with the vision of that ministry.

Let's look at 2 Chronicles 31:4 again. There was great revival in the land during Hezekiah's reign. The armies of Israel were victorious over their enemies and in destroying the sinful objects and practices of the land.

121

Hezekiah assigned priests and Levites to sing praises and give thanks offerings at the Temple to honor the Lord. But it also says that "the king contributed from his own possessions for the morning and evening burnt offerings and for the burnt offerings on the Sabbaths, New Moons and appointed feasts as written in the Law of the LORD" (2 Chronicles 31:3 NIV).

He then ordered the people to bring the priests and Levites their portion so they could devote themselves to the law of the Lord. Do you know how the people responded? "Azariah the chief priest, from the family of Zadok, answered, 'Since the people began to bring their contributions to the temple of the LORD, we have had enough to eat and plenty to spare, because the LORD has blessed his people, and this great amount is left over'" (2 Chronicles 31:10 NIV).

The people gave so joyfully that it was piled up in *heaps*! Their generosity and faithful giving helped keep the vision alive in the man of God and helped bring to pass all that he was called to do and more. As a result, the people continued to be blessed during Hezekiah's reign. I love how that chapter ends: "This is what Hezekiah did throughout Judah, doing what was good and right and faithful before the LORD his God. In everything that he undertook in the service of God's temple and in obedience to the law and the commands, he sought his God and worked wholeheartedly. And so he prospered" (2 Chronicles 31:20-21 NIV).

FIRST FRUITS AT WITHOUT WALLS

At the beginning of every year, in the month of January, Randy and I, along with our entire congregation, dedicate ourselves to a holy consecrated fast and the offering of first fruits. January is the first month of our year, and the *first* establishes the rest. We want to start our year with the discipline of fasting and consecrating ourselves to God. We also present our first fruits of the year to the Lord in the form of one day's salary, one week's salary, or even one whole month's salary as each person has the faith and ability to give.

Since I began to understand the power of the first fruits principle, I have never had a provision problem. Many of the significant things in my life happened out of first fruits or coming in obedience and alignment with the order of God. I know what it is to not even have two pennies to rub together. I've been so emotionally depressed and depleted at times in my life that it was an effort to muster up two positive thoughts. I know what it is to be down and out. I know what it is to have broken relationships. I know what it is for counselors to give up on you. I know what it is for life to label you. I know what it is to be depleted in almost every area of your life. But I also know what it is to get the revelation of this principle and find out that God has provided for me joy, peace, commitment, protection, safety, wellness, wholeness, relationship, provision, finances, to dream big and to live in abundance. Believe me, when you act in faith, trusting God that the root governs the rest, the life

God puts you into is bigger than the life you are living.

When we put God's will first in our lives, all else falls into place. Multiplication is released in our lives and in the lives of others. Remember the feeding of the 5000 in the wilderness? Jesus, the High Priest, received the offering of just five loaves of bread and two fish, and pronounced the blessing over it. Not only were His disciples fed, but so were more than 5000 men, women and children, with twelve baskets full left over (see Matthew 14:19-21).

CHAPTER 9

TRUCKLOAD OF TURKEYS

I could give you so many examples of how God's favor has manifested in our lives and ministry, and the lives of those in our congregation since we began to give first fruits, truly recognizing God in His proper place and order. One of the more unusual situations came as a result of an outreach we do each year at Thanksgiving called "A Table in the Wilderness." We set out a full banqueting table for those who are hungry...the homeless, single moms and others who are without.

When we initially started this outreach, we announced our plans to the congregation at Without Walls. They gave most of the food we needed, but we still desperately needed the all-important bird that is associated with this day of thanks. We had no turkeys, no money to go buy them, and the time for the banquet was drawing near.

While getting a haircut one day, Randy found himself in a conversation with a man at the salon. At one point, Randy began telling the man about our outreach, and how we still needed turkeys to feed the people. It was a divine appointment, because that man just happened to be a food distributor and had—get this—a truckload of frozen turkeys that he wanted to donate to someone for such a cause. That truck held nearly a thousand turkeys! It was an incredible blessing and outpouring of God's favor.

But we soon discovered that we had another problem...we didn't have a thousand ovens!

I met Randy later that day at the tiny "hole-in-the-wall" diner that we often frequented. The owner was this wonderful woman from New York who did everything from waiting her own tables, to preparing the food, to washing the dishes. She probably brought in just enough business to keep the bills paid. Of course, that's partially why we liked the place so much. We enjoyed blessing her, and, because not many people knew about the place, we liked that we could slip in and get a great deli sandwich in no time at all. We didn't realize that was all about to change.

When we walked in that day, the owner said, "Preacher, is there anything I can do for you?" And Randy said, "As a matter of fact, we need a few turkeys cooked." For the next several days, literally around the clock, the folks at that little diner cooked turkeys that would be used to bless those who had nothing.

We also gave turkeys to nearly every member of our congregation who would take one home to cook and bring back. Finally, this vast banquet came together. Hundreds were blessed and fed because of the favor of the Lord that year.

But the blessings did not stop there. The following week after the outreach we stopped back by the diner. As we pulled into the parking lot of our secluded little spot, we couldn't believe our eyes. There were cars everywhere! They were parked out front, along the side, and people were sitting in or on their cars reading menus from the diner. We couldn't figure out what was going on. We walked in and there were dishes piled up, and the owner was running around like crazy trying to get everyone served.

When Randy and I caught her eye, she said, "Preacher, you did this! Ever since I cooked those turkeys for you, look what has happened!" Her tiny business had exploded and she didn't even understand the principle of operating in God's favor.

OUR OFFICES

In chapter 4, I told you how God provided an abundant return on the first fruits offering we sowed from my speaking engagement at the Greek Orthodox Church. With the $15,000 gift we received the next day, we were able to rent a high school auditorium and finally begin having actual services. From there we relocated to a rented warehouse facility that included a "first option" for us to purchase the building if it went up for sale. The deal fell through, however, and we were once again looking for a facility.

Randy sent several of us out to "spy out the land" looking for other opportunities. I went to an area of town that was far from "up and coming." The specific area I was focusing on was run down and unused. In fact, it was the old stadium area, and at the time there was nothing to indicate life or prosperity. As I drove by, I saw one particular old brick building sitting off in the back. When I drove up to it I could see that it had been boarded up for some time. It had also been vandalized and had weeds growing up everywhere. But something else happened when I pulled up on that abandoned and distressed property. God clearly impressed to my heart saying, "This is your building." That word was enough for me. I went back to Randy and told him what I'd found.

Naturally, as I described this "wonderful find," his initial response was to ask if I was crazy. What would we do with an old abandoned office building? But once I convinced him that I truly believed I had heard from the Lord, he agreed to look into purchasing the property.

At that time we found out that it appraised for close to $4 million. That was way out of our $500,000 league—and even that would have required a lot of chicken-dinner fundraisers and applying for a loan. But Randy and I agreed that if God said it was ours, we would make an offer we could handle. He called the owners and offered $1.2 million—but they laughed at him and told him to call back when he was ready to make a *serious* offer.

A few weeks passed, and I still felt as strongly as ever that the property was to be ours. Somewhat reluctantly, but believing God's word, Randy agreed to call and check on it again. This time, we discovered that the property had been sold in a bulk auction! A bank in Atlanta had purchased most of the distressed properties in that area. But instead of allowing discouragement to take hold, we pressed in with even more determination, expecting God to turn what seemed to be a negative into a positive.

We were warned ahead of time that we'd never get

through to the man in charge of the particular property we wanted, especially since it was sold in bulk. But they obviously didn't calculate the one factor that makes all the difference: God's favor. We got directly through to that man, and what's more, he happened to have the deed and the paperwork for that property lying on his desk when we called. When we told him we were interested, he said, "Make me an offer." Now, in the natural, when you've already been turned down—and laughed at—for offering 1.2 million on a property valued at nearly $4 million, your instinct is to go a little higher. But not when God is involved!

Randy said, "We can offer you $600,000."

The man replied, "Done—but it has to be a cash-only deal, and you have thirty days."

Delighted and rejoicing over God's goodness, we agreed. We took all the money that we had in the bank, which was only about $100,000, and put it into escrow. Since we were only a young ministry there was no way we were going to get a loan, and we had no idea how to go about it anyway. So naturally, we began to fast and pray.

Approximately eighteen days later, a woman who had heard about the situation called us. We do not know how she knew all the details. She was not even a member of our church, and we had only met her once before that. Speaking with my husband she said, "How much do you need, four…five…six hundred thousand?"

My husband replied, "Yes!"

The woman answered, "Ok." And that was the end

of the conversation.

As the 30th day drew closer and closer, we continued to do everything we could—fundraising, fasting, marching, you name it. God gave us a specific word out of Psalm 121:3, "He will not allow your foot to slip or to be moved; He Who keeps you will not slumber" (NIV). We were encouraged to *stand*, and it would come to pass.

On day 29, the day before the closing was scheduled, the bank contacted us, concerned the deal would not go through. When the bank representative asked why the money was not yet in escrow, Randy said, "The money is being transferred. Don't worry, my Father has it and He is very wealthy."

The next day, as Randy and I were preparing to leave for the closing, that same woman who contacted us around the 18th day and asked what we needed, called to find out where and when the closing was to take place. We left for the closing, still not knowing how it was all going to come together, but we kept our faith in what God said. When we arrived, the woman met us there with a check for $630,000—enough to cover the entire purchase price as well as the closing costs!

The blessings of that property continue to multiply to this day in so many ways. In fact, the area has developed so much in the past five years that we now own some of the most prime real estate in Tampa, Florida.

HEDGED WITH FAVOR

Our lives have become a "favor walk" since learning to first fruit, putting God first in all things. I've never owned a business card, or tried to open any doors to make anything happen. But the favor of God is manifested, proving His covenant. Favor is undeserved access. It takes you places you may not be qualified to go otherwise. Only the favor of God can get you there.

Once we started Paula White Media Ministries, favor opened doors with several secular networks for specific appearances. Along the way I was told many times there was no way I would ever get on a large Christian network—so I didn't even try. I was not pursuing that option at all. But remember, our media ministry was birthed out of a first fruits offering. God's blessings were released and His favor was hedging us in. I believe that is why I received a phone call one day from a representative of that network. He was calling to inform me that the owner had been trying to make contact because they wanted to offer me a full program slot. A very close person within the network confirmed later that it was truly favor, because that just does not happen!

I always quote the scripture, "Blessed be the Lord, who daily loadeth us with benefits, even the God of our salvation" (Psalm 68:19). But I can't tell you how many people have said to me, "Paula, do you really believe that scripture you quote?" Yes, I do! I believe God for daily benefits to be loaded up in my life. Why? Because it has nothing at all to do with me. By *faith* I am positioned in right standing with God and in the order of God. Our ministry was birthed with first fruits, and the favor of the Lord has never lifted. Just like that truckload of turkeys to feed the hungry, the blessings have been running over in my personal life…and for so many others who have begun to make the principle of first fruits a part of their lives.

FIRST FRUITS OPENS DOORS

Beverly is a wonderful, faithful woman of God. After serving on the mission field for about four years, she sensed the Lord's direction to return to the states. Beverly relocated to Atlanta, Georgia, intending to live there for about a year. She moved in with a friend for a short time, but quickly went through the $400 she had to get started. Finding a job was imperative. With a background in human resources, she sought something in that field, only to find herself working at a car dealership selling cars instead. But God was with her. Though she had never sold cars before in her life, she became the top salesperson on the floor a short time after she began. Beverly had a few debts from the past, and because she'd been overseas, some of those debts had even gone into collection and creditors were beginning to harass her. Beverly said,

> "I began to think about the fact that, if
> I was going to spend a year in Georgia,
> working and living there, I needed to

think about sowing seed. So I began to pray and ask God for His guidance. Tithing I understood, but I also knew that, at the beginning of the year, you give a first fruits offering. So after praying to God about this very thing, I saw Paula White talking about first fruits in a televised message. Even though I had not had the opportunity to give a significant first fruits offering for some time because I was not working, I did understand the importance of it. So I asked God if I was to sow into her ministry. December was my best month at the dealership, so my first fruits offering of my first check of the coming year was going to be the best offering I had ever given. I felt the Holy Spirit direct me to sow the seed into Paula White's ministry.

Through my dealings at the local bank, I had come to know the bank manager rather well. She offered me a position at the bank, which I accepted. I started paying off debts. I realized that the offering I gave was not just to bless me financially. It was an offering that opened doors and gave me insight and understanding. First fruits is one of the

> hardest things to do, because you are just
> taking the whole thing and saying 'God,
> here it is…I trust You to manage it for
> me,' and He does! It was like God said,
> 'Because you have entrusted Me with
> the responsibility for your year, your life
> and your livelihood, I am going to show
> you things and make things known to
> you that are important to your
> well being.'"

When God gives you revelation, that revelation causes you to move out in faith. When revelation hits your spirit, you don't just sit in the boat and watch everybody else walk on water. You say to yourself, "If they can walk on water, so can I!" Start calling those things that are not as though they are. Start speaking the fact that everything you need has already been provided—all godliness and all spiritual blessings have already been given to you. You just need to walk in it.

During the days of Elijah, there was a widow who lived in a town called Zarephath. A severe famine fell over the land because there had been no rain for crops or herds. So naturally, that is where God sent His prophet.

> When [Elijah] came to the town gate, a
> widow was there gathering sticks. He
> called to her and asked, "Would you
> bring me a little water in a jar so I may

have a drink?" As she was going to get it, he called, "And bring me, please, a piece of bread."

"As surely as the LORD your God lives," she replied, "I don't have any bread—only a handful of flour in a jar and a little oil in a jug. I am gathering a few sticks to take home and make a meal for myself and my son, that we may eat it—and die."

Elijah said to her, "Don't be afraid. Go home and do as you have said. But first make a small cake of bread for me from what you have and bring it to me, and then make something for yourself and your son" (1 Kings 17:10-13 NIV).

Can you *imagine*?! Elijah would seem rather audacious, but you have to understand…he was operating under revelation. God had already told Him that He had commanded a widow in Zarephath to provide for him. That part is easy to understand. But what would make that poor widow—who had conceded that she and her young son were to suffer death by starvation over the coming days—give *any* of what she had to a stranger? Revelation.

Elijah told her not to be afraid because, "The LORD, the God of Israel, says: 'The jar of flour will not be used up and the jug of oil will not run dry until the day the

LORD gives rain on the land'" (1 Kings 17:14 NIV). In the face of despair, that widow woman suddenly got revelation from the man of God. He told her to give her first fruits—even though she had next to nothing—to him, and she would receive the blessings of God. She was reminded to put God first and she willingly obeyed, bringing Elijah the water and cake he'd requested. As a result of her first fruits offering, "there was food every day for Elijah and for the woman and her family. For the jar of flour was not used up and the jug of oil did not run dry, in keeping with the word of the LORD spoken by Elijah" (1 Kings 17:15-16 NIV).

No matter what situation you may be in, you have the Word of the Lord just as this widow woman did. Not only has your "truckload of turkeys" been provided—the cooks have been provided as well! Your oil and flour do not have to run out. When you give your first fruits, the blessings of the Lord *will* be poured out in your life. Let that revelation get into your spirit and motivate you to new levels of faith!

CHAPTER 10

LIVING IN THE BLESSING

God "rested" on the seventh day of creation, not because He was tired, but by example. He was setting into motion His desire that man experience restoration, replenishment, and refreshment. God designed us to work six days and rest one. He designed us to have a rhythm in our lives in which we have a time totally devoted to restoring what has been given out, replenishing what has been used up, receiving back what has been spent, and refreshing what has grown stale. He designed us so that our deepest form of restoration, replenishment and refreshment is to come in relationship to Him.

You will live in the blessings of God when you determine to follow His principles. Start now to establish the pattern for your family that the first thing you do on the first day of every week is go to the house of the Lord to honor and worship Him. Set time aside on the Sabbath to study His Word, putting knowledge of His Word in the first place in your life. Seek first His kingdom by giving God the first moments of each day, thereby establishing how the rest of your day will go. Give to God what is His—the first of all things, and the tithe. The first check from a new job, the first of the year's salary, and so on. Your first fruits offering might be a day, it might be a week, it might be a month.

Remember (*zakar*) God as *first* in all things. When you bring your life into alignment with what the Word of God says about you, then you will find the pattern of *your* life. We see God as being all-powerful, all-wise, all-loving and eternal. But we should also see Him as our Rock among the shifting sands of life. See Him as the Balm of Gilead in the midst of your sickness. See Him as your Provider in the midst of your lack. When you first fruits the Lord, you are positioning yourself for just that! As David wrote, "I said to the LORD, 'You are my Lord; apart from you I have no good thing'" (Psalm 16:2 NIV).

As I've said before, God does not look at your past mistakes and exclude you from His promises. Neither does God give you His promises on the basis of any good works you have done. I've said it before: the first fruits offering is not about "winning" God's favor, but about "releasing" it—acting in faith in order to see it manifest in your life. It is a principle, not simply an offering. It is your faith in Him that brings God's promises to you. God doesn't look at your resume. He isn't impressed with your cuteness or cleverness. As you present God with the offering of the first, entrusting Him with the rest, I know without a shadow of a doubt that God has great things to be released to you! If you will give God your faith, He will give you your future. "For the LORD God is a sun and shield; the LORD bestows favor and honor; no good thing does he withhold from those whose walk is blameless" (Psalm 84:11 NIV).

STORIES OF FIRSTS

Putting God first in the morning has changed North Carolinian Wendy's life. She heard the teaching on first

141

fruits and began to practice it. She writes, "I have been spending time every morning with God and have been truly blessed." She also gave her first financial first fruits offering. Just seven days later she received an abundance of groceries—that she could not afford—from people who had no idea how desperate her situation happened to be.

A precious member of our congregation let us know recently how promotion manifested in her life after giving two weeks pay as her first fruits offering in January. On January 30, she was called into the office at her corporate health job and asked if she was interested in receiving a promotion to a higher position than she currently held. She was offered a $4000 increase in pay starting the following week.

Linda from Texas suffered from hepatitis of the liver for 32 years. She began the year recently by sowing her entire disability check as a first fruits offering. A few months later she went back to her doctor. He said, "I don't know what happened!" They could not find any trace of the virus in her body. This is the second year of giving her first fruits offering.

Anthony from Nassau wrote to tell us how he had seen my teaching on first fruits. Revelation hit his heart—but he truly had no money. Anthony had been unemployed for five months. So he decided to pray. "Lord," he said, "if you want me to give a first fruits offering, you will need to send me the money." Already, Anthony acknowledged that he had no ability to get wealth outside of God's provision—and God did indeed provide. Anthony gave a first fruits offering of $900, an amount he felt would adequately represent one week of pay from a job he *did not yet* have. His check arrived at our offices on the first of February. We found out later that the very next day, February 2, a gentleman at his church who is a CEO asked Anthony to call him because he had a brand new job for him. But that's not all. The new job paid four times what his first fruits offering represented per month! Anthony now says, "First fruits is awesome!"

Shardohn of Virginia had never heard the scripture found in Romans 11:16 that reads, "If the part of the dough offered as firstfruits is holy, then the whole batch is holy; if the root is holy, so are the branches." But that one scripture opened her eyes to the principle of first fruits this past January. She writes, "I had a financial need for my rent so I was a little nervous about giving first fruits, but I did not let that stop me. I gave my first fruits offering of $1000.00. My faith came by hearing the word of God and God used this opportunity to show off on my behalf. Now I work only three days per week and the Lord has allowed me to make more money than I did when I was full time. Now I get to spend more time with my family. How exciting! Also my real estate business, and other business ventures are beginning to blossom. To God be the Glory. God cannot fail!"

The blessings of God come in so many different forms. Julia wrote to tell us, "Last year my husband and

I gave of our first paychecks for a first fruit. During the year, we have been doubly blessed, I gave birth to two beautiful twin girls and my husband has been shown tremendous favor by his boss. I believe all this blessing was due to our faithfulness on giving first fruit. Thank you for being willing to teach on such a controversial subject, we have been blessed because of your faithfulness."

A couple from Pennsylvania were determined to pay off their credit card debts and had established a plan to do so over a 15-month period. After hearing the teaching on first fruits, faith rose up in their hearts, and they knew God would honor their obedience. So they gave their first fruits offering in January, and were able to pay their large credit card debts off in just 6 months. The wife's name is Paula, and she writes, "We also were able to take two paid-for vacations to spend with family. I was able to attend the Paula White Alive Conference with my girl-friend. We were able to save a small nest egg to have money saved for emergencies in the future. And my hus-band was given a new job with better pay, and wonderful opportunity for growth and professional development with a financially strong company. It is amazing to see the Lord's blessing beginning to overtake us. We are truly thankful to God for giving us the opportunity to give our first fruits offering!"

Shannon from North Carolina writes, "I have to thank you for your teachings on first fruits. We are avid tithers and give special offerings, however, we had never heard of 'first fruits.' Everything you said was backed up by Scripture. So, we sowed our first fruits offering with the faith and belief that God would use it to His glory, and would bless us. Never in our imagination did we think He would bless us like He did. My husband just received a huge promotion and his salary was increased almost 30%, which is unheard of! We will have to relocate, but we are so excited just thinking about how God is going to use us."

Many of these first fruits offerings—one week and two weeks pay—may seem large. God says that all first fruits belong to Him, great or small. He honors the faith you demonstrate in giving Him the "firsts." Deirdre from Detroit can testify to this fact. She gave all she had—$18.00—to the Lord in a first fruits offering. Six-months later she was running her own mortgage business. Not only that, a few months later God blessed her with office space in downtown Detroit in the heart of the financial district. She had favor with a local radio station, receiving a month of 30-minute radio spots for the price of 30-second spots, with the potential to reach 4 million people. Her national managers were so impressed with her progress, the following year she was asked to meet with the owner of the company. She said, "I never thought that my life would change from earning $18 a week to meeting with a billionaire."

After hurricane Katrina devastated New Orleans, Louisiana, Tammara was among those who lost absolutely everything. She was evacuated to Texas, and began to make her home there. She had received no money from FEMA, and she had no insurance on her Louisiana home or belongings. The only income she received was an unemployment check. She trusted our ministry as a place to give her first fruits offering and gave her unemployment check, a total of $98. Just one week later she received a check for $2,196.

Presenting an offering of one week's salary was truly a sacrifice for Susan in New Mexico. But she understood the principle of faith behind first fruits, and gave her offering to our ministry. She wrote to tell us that she received a new job with an $18,000 a year increase in salary the following March. "God is so faithful," she writes. "I am sowing my first fruits offering again this year. Praise God!"

"Praise the Lord for miracles," begins the letter we received from Janika of Rhode Island. She continued, "As soon as I sent my first fruits offering, I received a phone call from my lawyer. He called to notify me that I had finally received the settlement from my case which had been on hold for over two years." She had lost hope for receiving any money from this case. But the first fruits offering truly opens doors!

FOR A PURPOSE

David said, "The LORD knoweth the days of the upright: and their inheritance shall be for ever. They shall not be ashamed in the evil time: and in the days of famine they shall be satisfied" (Psalm 37:18-19). We have established that it is the first fruits offering that "gives you the power to get wealth," (Deuteronomy 8:18 NKJV). By "first fruiting" the Lord, putting Him in the proper place in your life, you release the promises of His blessings. But those blessings serve a purpose. When we are blessed, God is magnified and establishes His covenant with His people.

In Egypt, the Israelites had gone from an extremely prosperous nation to an oppressed people in slavery after 400 years. Pharaoh had even begun to kill the firstborn Israelite boys in an attempt to dwindle their numbers. They had nothing. But when God delivered His people, "The Israelites did as Moses instructed and asked the Egyptians for articles of silver and gold and for clothing. The LORD had made the Egyptians favorably disposed toward the people, and they gave them what they asked for; so they plundered the Egyptians" (Exodus 12:35-3 NIV). He gave them favor and three million Israelites walked out of that rich land with an abundance of gold and valuables. According to Deuteronomy, God blessed them in order to establish His covenant.

Later, as Moses stood in the presence of the Lord receiving specific instructions as to how to use the plunder of gold and silver that they had taken, at the bottom of the mountain the people had decided to use their wealth to fashion an idol of gold that they could worship (see Exodus 32:2-4). That was not God's purpose for blessing His people. God gives us the ability to get wealth for a *purpose*. I have often said that your money has a mission. Money without purpose is materialism. We are to leave our children with an inheritance. We are to enjoy a portion of the fruit of our labor. The Word of God clearly shows us how to manage and distribute the money with which we have been entrusted. We have a mission to spread the news of His Kingdom, and the gospel of the Lord Jesus.

The final testimony I want to share with you is so colorful, and such an example of this very thing. It comes from a woman named Sarah, who lives in Eaton, Colorado. She starts her letter with the statement, "The Lord's timing is always right." Sarah understands that the first fruits offering is about the principle that establishes the pattern of breakthroughs and blessings in your life. She had been looking to purchase land with a house, or a place she could build for some time. She had a large down payment saved in the bank, and had been pre-qualified for a large mortgage loan, but could not find the right place. Then the Lord told her to give her entire down payment as a first fruits offering. That was on the eighth of January. The very next day, her friend was passing through the town of Eaton when she saw a site so peculiar she called Sarah to tell her about it. She said, "A very large squirrel was struggling to cross the road carrying a large ear of yellow corn in his mouth."

Her friend was laughing at this strange sight when she noticed that there was a for sale sign on the 'bed & breakfast' just across the street. Sarah continued, "I had a vision in 1978 about a house the Lord wanted to use for His people." She asked her friend if the house was yellow with a wrap-around porch. It was. She asked if it had a swing on the porch, facing west. It did. She asked if it had a large blue spruce in the front yard. Of course, it did. Sarah became ecstatic.

She went to see the house as soon as she could. Once she laid eyes on it, she knew it was indeed the great Victorian house she had seen in a vision so many years ago. But there was a problem: She'd given her entire down payment as a first fruits offering!

The favor of God allowed her to qualify for a 100% mortgage on the property and she moved in that February. Almost a year later, the Lord told her that someone was coming to pay off the mortgage. Upon receiving that word from the Lord, like the widow of Zarephath acting on the revelation of God's provision, Sarah sowed another offering to see even greater breakthroughs based on God's promise.

The 'bed & breakfast' is now called "The Secret Place," and is a place, every second Friday of the month, for Christians from all over Colorado and Nebraska to gather and spend the night. She writes that they are experiencing "an open heaven like the Brownsville Revival. Some drive for hours to be here, and people are healed and delivered. In addition to the outpouring of the Holy Spirit, people enjoy the peace that surpasses understanding at The Secret Place."

I will hear what God the LORD will

speak: for he will speak peace unto his people, and to his saints: but let them not turn again to folly. Surely his salvation is nigh them that fear him; that glory may dwell in our land (Psalm 85:8-9).

JUST LIVE IT!

You cannot prepare yourself in a day. You must prepare yourself every day...day after day...for the rest of your days. As Hebrews tells us, "Remember your leaders, who spoke the word of God to you. Consider the outcome of their way of life and imitate their faith. Jesus Christ is the same yesterday and today and forever" (Hebrews 13:7-8 NIV). Many have gone before us who have learned to have faith in God's principle of first fruits. I encourage you to step out into the knowledge you now have, and do the same. As David said:

> Your promises have been thoroughly tested, and your servant loves them. Though I am lowly and despised, I do not forget your precepts. Your righteousness is everlasting and your law is true. Trouble and distress have come upon me, but your commands are my delight. Your statutes are forever right; give me understanding that I may live (Psalm 119:140-144 NIV).

150

The one day, one week, or one month first fruits offering is just one step—work out your faith—believe day after day that God has seen your offering of first fruits and blessed the rest. Now live in the blessing for generations to come! God has given you the "blue print"—the pattern to follow in order to release what He has provided for you: abundant life!

Learn even more about how

First Fruits

*can yield incredible
blessings in your life!*

Paula has prepared an additional, in-depth resource for you on the life-changing biblical principle of first fruits. In a special 2-disc set with CD and companion DVD, Paula goes deep into the Word to reveal the steps you can take to release God's hand of unlimited anointing, blessing and prosperity into your life.

Unlock **YOUR POTENTIAL**
and live your life according
to **GOD'S GRAND DESIGN**!

"Become my Covenant Partner and let me show you the

practical, God-given principles you need to receive all

that the Master Builder has planned for your life."

Paula White

AS A PAULA WHITE MINISTRIES **COVENANT PARTNER**, you can join Paula in reaching millions through television and outreach ministries. Your faithful prayers and giving will literally transform lives. But the life most impacted will be your own. As a life coach and pastor, Paula will teach you how to begin living in abundant blessings and divine purpose.

BECOME A **COVENANT PARTNER** TODAY
AND RECEIVE THESE **2007 PARTNERSHIP BENEFITS**:

- **2007 LIFE BY DESIGN DAILY PLANNER.** This beautifully designed daily resource (available in either eggplant or saddle colors) will be a constant reminder of the potential and purpose inside of you. You will find words of encouragement and Scripture to help you maximize every single day! This 188-page daily planner is beautifully gold-edged with ribbon and also contains different types of prayers for specific situations in life, a one-year Bible reading schedule, three-year calendar and plenty of room for your thoughts and notes.

- **IN-DEPTH MONTHLY TEACHINGS ON CD**, available upon request, are selected exclusively for Covenant Partners to challenge you and keep you growing in your destiny!

- **EXCLUSIVE INTERNET ACCESS** to Covenant Partner features on our ministry website and, to keep our web address handy, a decorative mouse pad emblazoned with our ministry logo.

- **YOUR EXCLUSIVE COVENANT PARTNER MEMBERSHIP CARD** for preferred seating at ministry-sponsored events and a 20% discount on most Paula White Ministries resources!

FOR MORE INFORMATION on how to receive your beautiful Life by Design Daily Planner and other Covenant Partner benefits for 2007, go to **www.paulawhite.org**!

NOTES

NOTES

NOTES

NOTES